HAVRE DE GRACE
IN THE
WAR OF 1812

D1194731

HAVRE DE GRACE

IN THE

WAR OF 1812

Fire on the Chesapeake

HEIDI L. GLATFELTER

FOREWORD BY DAVID R. CRAIG

Charleston London

THE
History
PRESS

Published by The History Press
Charleston, SC 29403
www.historypress.net

Cover image: This famous image of the British plundering and burning Havre de Grace endures and shows firsthand the destruction the British caused. The building on fire to the left is Mrs. Sears's tavern. Notice the British pilfering a dresser and baby cradle and stealing a coach by loading it on one of their ships. British Lieutenant George Westphal, who was shot in the hand by a townsperson during the attack, stands in the middle. *Brown University Library.*
Back Cover, top: National Park Service/© Gerry Embleton.

First published 2013

Manufactured in the United States

ISBN 978.1.60949.633.3

Library of Congress CIP data applied for.

CONTENTS

FOREWORD

Havre de Grace is Maryland's second-oldest and nineteenth-largest municipality. Our first president, George Washington, and our current president, Barack Obama, both passed through it to get to the nation's capital.

General Rochambeau's army camped there on its way to the Battle of Yorktown, which ended the American Revolutionary War. It was an important path for enslaved African Americans on the Underground Railroad and a chance for freedom.

Located at the head of the Chesapeake Bay, it provides a wonderful view of America's largest estuary. At the mouth of the Susquehanna River, it is at the end of the largest river east of the Mississippi—444 miles south of Cooperstown, New York. The newest connection between those two cities is Cal Ripken Jr., born in Havre de Grace and enshrined in the Baseball Hall of Fame.

Its most tragic day, however, occurred on May 3, 1813, when a British fleet commanded by Rear Admiral Cockburn landed marines and troops here. The plundering and burning of the buildings and terror experienced by its citizens is excellently portrayed by Heidi L. Glatfelter.

Heidi spells out the history of the city before that date (luckily it did not become the nation's capital, which experienced the same disaster a year later), tells us about the people there (including a fifteen-year-old heroine) and concludes with the aftermath.

The two decades following the attack saw the city virtually disappear as it struggled to rebuild. But, as Heidi points out, Havre de Grace became an important industrial area and continues to grow.

Havre de Grace in the War of 1812: Fire on the Chesapeake fills a void that has existed for some time when people read about this first war of the United States as a free nation. Reading Ms. Glatfelter's work will help anyone who does not live here better understand the beauty, history and resilience of Havre de Grace.

David R. Craig
Harford County Executive

ACKNOWLEDGEMENTS

This book would not have been possible without the wonderful residents of Havre de Grace, Maryland, both past and present. I thank them all for allowing me to step into their world and tell their story. I also must thank the staff at The History Press and my editor, Hannah Cassilly, for their support and guidance.

This book grew out of an exhibit project grant written by the late Brenda Guldenzopf, and without her leadership and drive, it would never have gotten off the ground. Even though I never had the chance to meet her, I owe her my gratitude. The grant Brenda wrote allowed the various history museums in Havre de Grace to come together and tell the story of the British attack on their town. (Come see the exhibits on display at each of the Havre de Grace museums through 2014!) The staff and volunteers of these museums have worked tirelessly on this project since 2010 and have allowed me to work beside them as the project manager. Much of their work informs this book. These fine people include Danyelle Dorsey Rickard and Charlie Vasilakis at the Susquehanna Museum at the Lock House; Bethany Baker and James Dryden of the Concord Point Lighthouse; Darlene Perry and Phil Barker of the Havre de Grace Maritime Museum; C. John Sullivan, Pat Vincenti and Mindy Elledge of the Havre de Grace Decoy Museum; Cindi Beane and Helene Klair of the Chesapeake Heritage Conservancy; Brigitte Peters of the Havre de Grace Visitor's Center; and Linda Noll and Angela Yau of the Steppingstone Museum, as well as the boards of directors of all these organizations.

ACKNOWLEDGEMENTS

I also extend my thanks to others who have worked on this project and aided me with information: Dianne Klair, Mitch Shank, Ellsworth Shank, William Allen, Bill Martin, Mitch Mitchell, Bill MacIntire, Bob Magee, Martha Jacksteit, Cecil Hill, George DeHority, Dick Klair and the project historians, Christopher George and Mike Dixon.

I am indebted to Richard Sherrill, James Chrismer and the other volunteers at the Historical Society of Harford County, as well as the archivists at the Maryland Historical Society, for their help with resources and images.

I thank the funders of the grant project—the National Park Service and the Maryland Heritage Areas Authority—and their staff people, Abbi Wicklein-Bayne and Kate Marks at the Park Service and Jennifer Ruffner at the Heritage Area Authority. I thank Havre de Grace mayor Wayne Dougherty and the city council for their support, and I thank Harford County executive David R. Craig for his enthusiastic backing of the grant project and for agreeing to write the foreword of this book.

A special thanks is owed to Peter Harrington at the Brown University Library, who provided the cover art for this book free of charge. I would also like to thank my friends, my loving family—Perry, Lois and Wendy Glatfelter—and Joe Schlag for his unwavering understanding and support.

INTRODUCTION

Havre de Grace is known today for its beautiful waterfront setting, quaint historic area, charming bed-and-breakfasts, handcrafted decoys and bustling restaurants, museums and shops. Havre de Grace was designated as a town in 1785, but the area's storied history is documented as far back as 1607, only a few months after the English settled their first colony at Jamestown.

However, it wasn't until the fateful morning of May 3, 1813, that the town ensured its inclusion in the history books. The sun hadn't even risen when the British came ashore to ravage and burn the city as part of their Chesapeake campaign during the War of 1812. Many of the things that make Havre de Grace a tourist destination today made it a target for the British two hundred years ago.

But Havre de Grace rose from the ashes and rebuilt. Today, it boasts an eclectic collection of historic buildings, although most date from the mid- to late nineteenth century, thanks to the British burning of the eighteenth-century structures. Also remaining are the stories of the day the British attacked, in the form of three first-person accounts. They tell of the atrocities perpetrated on Havre de Grace's civilians and the heroes who rose to the town's defense.

As the 200th anniversary of the War of 1812 approached, the townspeople of Havre de Grace sought a way to remember those who had lived in this town on May 3, 1813, and rebuilt it to the thriving waterside village it is today. Led by Marsha Jacksteit and the late Brenda Guldenzopf, the six museums in town partnered with the Visitor's Center and the City of

Havre de Grace government to obtain two grants: one from the National Park Service and one from the Maryland Heritage Areas Authority.

These grants funded community history research, exhibits, wayside signage, educational materials and a scale model of 1813 Havre de Grace. I was fortunate enough to be hired as the project manager for the grant implementation, which resulted in my becoming thoroughly engrossed in the story of that fateful day in 1813.

The exhibits and other materials being created by the grant committee will go far to educate the public on the attack on Havre de Grace. However, by the nature of their medium, exhibit panels can only contain about two hundred words and will only be on display for a year or two. I felt this compelling story should also be documented in book form in order to preserve the extensive research work the committee has done on the project and to stimulate future research on questions that remain unanswered from the day the British came ashore at Havre de Grace.

Another of my goals as I wrote this book was to weave together the three surviving first-person accounts of the attack. I was able to glean much information from each work individually, but it was only when I started to combine them that the story of 1813 Havre de Grace—its citizens, its buildings, its tradespeople, its governments—came to life. Newspaper articles, letters and research from other historians helped to round things out.

As the anniversary of the War of 1812 in Maryland marches on, it is important to recognize not just the high-profile success of the Battle of Baltimore but also the citizens of small towns who experienced the terrorizing force of the British navy. In most written accounts of the War of 1812, the attack on Havre de Grace merits only a paragraph, if it is mentioned at all. In order to fully appreciate what the townspeople of Havre de Grace experienced on May 3, 1813, an entire book is required. We will begin about four hundred years ago.

Finding Havre de Grace

In April 1607, three ships from Europe—the *Susan Constant, Godspeed* and *Discovery*—landed on Virginia's shores, carrying 105 passengers to start Jamestown, the first English colony here in the New World. (This was years before the Pilgrims landed on Plymouth Rock in modern-day Massachusetts.) With them was John Smith, who would, within a year, be one of the first Europeans to set foot on the land that was to become Havre de Grace.

The settlers' first years at Jamestown were a great challenge. The all-male group struggled to get crops in the ground and shelters built. Most were unaccustomed to hard work, having not experienced it in England. Their lackadaisical attitude, combined with Virginia's humid weather, poor drinking water and illnesses that had plagued them during their sea crossing, resulted in the death of more than half the group within the first year. Adding to their difficulties were the Powhatan Indian tribes on whom their arrival had intruded. The Native Americans were not pleased to be sharing their land and led many attacks against the English to make this point.

Leading the settlers in Jamestown was Captain John Smith. Many historians credit Smith "with almost singlehandedly preserving the first English Virginians from the ravages of their own sloth as well as from the hostility of their native neighbors."[1] The settlement managed to survive its first year in North America, and in the summer of 1608, Smith and a group of men set out to explore the Chesapeake region. They were searching for the two things that had brought Europeans to America in the first place: gold and silver, as well as a water passage across North America that would "enable them to reach China—where great profits awaited—without having to sail around Africa and across the Indian Ocean."[2]

It was on Smith's second voyage up the Chesapeake to explore that body of water and its river offshoots that he and the explorers happened upon the land we know today as Havre de Grace. Of course, as in Jamestown, Smith did not encounter uninhabited land. The Indian tribes living in the upper Chesapeake water basin were Susquehannocks, and Smith recorded his impressions of the warriors in his diary:

> *Upon this river inhabit a people called Susquehannock. 60 of those Susquehannocks came to [us] with skins, bows, arrows, targets, beads, swords, and tobacco pipes for presents. Such great and well proportioned men are seldom seen, for they seemed like giants to the English…Their attire is the skins of bears and wolves; some have cassocks made of bear heads and skins that a man's neck goes through the skin's neck…One had the head of a wolf hanging in a chain for a jewel, his tobacco pipe three quarters of a yard long, prettily carved with a bird, a bear, a deer, or some*

This map by Henricus Hondius is based on John Smith's landmark map from 1612. On the right side is a sketch of a Native American. Nova Virginiae Tabula, 1630.

such device at the great end, sufficient to beat out the brains of a man, with bows and arrows and clubs suitable to their greatness and conditions.[3]

An analysis of Smith's description not only tells us about the Susquehannocks as physical specimens but also sheds light on the types of natural resources available in the Upper Bay during the early seventeenth century. There were obviously bears, wolves, deer and birds in the area to eat, and the Indians had bows, arrows and swords for both hunting and defense.

From another passage in Smith's diary, we also know that the rivers were well stocked with oysters and finfish. Smith writes: "Abundance of fish lying so thicke with their heads above the water, as for want of nets, our barge running against them, we attempted to catch them in frying pans... no more variety for small fish had any one of us seene in any place."[4]

We also learn much about the Susquehannocks through descriptions in George Alsop's diary, although he wrote about sixty years later than Smith. Alsop, who lived in the Upper Bay area in the 1660s, provides detailed accounts of the Native Americans' lives:

The Women are the Butchers, Cooks, and Tillers of the ground, the Men think it below the honour of a Masculine, to stoop to any thing but that which their Gun, or Bow and Arrows can command. The Men kill the several Beasts which they meet withall in the Woods, and the Women are the Pack horses to fetch it in upon their backs, fleying and dressing the bydes, (as well as the flesh for provision) to make them fit for Trading, and which are brought down to the English at several seasons in the year, to truck and dispose of them for course Blankets, Guns, Powder and lead, Beads, small Looking-glasses, Knives, and Razors.[5]

Alsop, like Smith, also comments on the superior physical appearance of the Susquehannocks, saying they are "the most Noble and Heroick Nation of Indians that dwell upon the confines of America." He continues by saying they are "a people cast into the mould of a most large and Warlike deportment, the men being for the most part seven foot high in latitude, and in magnitude and bulk suitable to so high a pitch; their voyce large and hollow, as ascending out of a Cave, their gate and behavior strait, stately and majestick."[6]

After Smith met the Susquehannocks on August 6 and 7, 1608, he sailed back to Jamestown, where he was needed to keep the peace in the fledgling colony. He promised the tribe he would return the following year to visit but was unable to keep that promise and instead returned to England in 1609 after sustaining an injury.

Smith continued to promote the colonization of the New World through his writing from England. His descriptions of the upper Chesapeake Bay region drew Edward Palmer to the area, where he established a trading post in 1616 on what he named Palmer's Island. (Palmer's Island lies between present-day Havre de Grace and Perryville and supports the Route 40 bridge.) He and the two hundred men and women who lived on the island had success buying pelts from the Susquehannocks and reselling them to the Virginia colonists. But the settlement faded for unknown reasons, and nothing was left when Englishmen next visited the island in 1638 except for a couple of books.

Like Smith, Palmer explored the Chesapeake Bay area before Maryland was even a colony. In 1632, Lord Baltimore received a charter from English King Charles I to settle the colony of Maryland, named for Queen Henrietta Maria. However, the first governor of the colony, Leonard Calvert, and his men didn't arrive on the shores of Maryland until 1634, and they didn't sail up the Bay until twenty-four years later, in 1658. It was at this time that people received the first land grants in the Upper Bay, and the land that was to become Havre de Grace was granted to Godfrey Harmer.

First Landing of Leonard Calvert in Maryland. Oil on canvas by David Acheson Woodward, circa 1865–70. *Maryland Historical Society (MDHS).*

"Records indicated that the original Harmer deed... covered a section that ran from modern-day Concord Point at the southern end to the current location of the Amtrak Railroad Bridge at the northern one, a point opposite the southern edge of Palmer Island. Most of modern downtown Havre de Grace would have been included."[7]

By 1659, Harmer's land had been reassigned to Captain Thomas Stockett and became known as Stockett's Town. "Captain Stockett and his family should be given credit as the founders of the community. During the thirty years of their ownership, Stockett's Town grew from a remote outpost to a small center of commerce."[8]

George Alsop, 1666.

George Alsop, who wrote his impressions of the Susquehannock Indians, was an indentured servant of the Stocketts. Indentured servants were generally poor agricultural workers who, in order to escape England, signed a contract binding themselves to work for a landowner for a period of seven years. Indentured servants composed about three-quarters of the population of Maryland during the seventeenth century. Alsop's diaries contain a wealth of information about early Maryland, and besides writing about the Native Americans, he also included much about European life in the Upper Bay area.

Alsop records how beautiful and bountiful the Maryland area was, saying:

> *Pleasant, in respect of the multitude of Navigable Rivers and Creeks that conveniently and most profitably lodge within the armes of her green, spreading, and delightful Woods; whose natural womb (by her plenty) maintains and preserves the several diversities of Animals that rangingly inhabit her Woods; as she doth otherwise generously fructifie this piece of Earth with almost all sorts of Vegetables, as well Flowers with their varieties of colours and smells, as Herbes and Roots with their several effects and operative virtues, that offer their benefits daily to supply the want*

of the Inhabitant whene're their necessities shall Sub-poena *them to wait on their commands.*[9]

Despite the idyllic setting and plentiful natural resources, life for the Maryland Upper Bay colonists during this time was hard. "Words such as crude and harsh best describe Chesapeake society in the seventeenth century, and the county's citizens lived lives devoid of any but the most basic of material goods."[10]

During this period, most residents of the Upper Bay area were farmers and lived several miles from neighboring farms. "The average American rural dweller and his wife worked hard and were independent, self-respecting, and resourceful. These were qualities molded by the extremes of climate and the fact that they could be cut off from the rest of the country for months at a time."[11]

The chief crops in the Upper Bay were tobacco, corn and wheat, which were often shipped to England. The fathers and sons would work in the fields from daybreak until dark, while the mothers and daughters saw to the sewing of clothes, cooking of food, preserving and canning for winter and making of candles, soap, butter, cheese and other food items. Families of eight to thirteen children were common because there was so much work to do.

Hard work would also go into every meal. However, "the diet was not...altogether bad on farms. Most of them had a 'sarse' patch where vegetables were grown, and there was an abundance of milk, butter, and cheese. The mainstay of the family...was the pork-barrel, but beef was also used a great deal. A good dinner consisted of boiled pork and potatoes, or salt beef, turnips, and stewed pumpkins."[12] Of course, in Havre de Grace, people had access to fish and fowl and likely ate much more fresh meat than other colonists who did not have direct access to a major waterway.

In *The History of Harford County*, author Walter Preston paints a descriptive picture of home life:

> *There was little to be seen in the household that was not the product of the soil. In every home could be found a spinning wheel, and the housewife, besides her other duties, did the weaving of the material used for clothing, with the aid of her daughters; and around the open fire in the long winter evenings their deft fingers plied the knitting needles. The furniture was of the simplest kind and stoves were unknown. Candles or the roaring fire served the purpose of lighting the room...Traveling was done on horseback or in lumbering vehicles, and visits along the water were made in boats.*[13]

In 1666, during the Stocketts' ownership of the town, the Maryland colonial assembly passed an act that called for the construction of roads to connect to the rivers in order to facilitate travel and trade between the colonies. The creation of roads enabled farmers who rarely left their parcels of land to begin traveling between farms, shipping their goods to market and trading with other farmers.

Of course, to join the middle colonies of Virginia and Maryland to the northern colonies, a road had to cross the Susquehanna River. Stockett's Town was one point for crossing via a ferry service. Edward Jackson was the first of many ferry operators to transport travelers across the waterway. He set up a private ferry operation on the east side of the river and charged travelers exorbitant fees to cross to Stockett's Town on the west shore.

Europeans continued to develop the land around the Upper Bay, growing crops to sell at market now that it was easier to transport them to port. However, the interactions between the Susquehannocks and the Europeans in the area took a tremendous toll on the Indians. Smallpox, a disease carried by the Europeans for which the Indians had no immunity, ripped through Susquehannock tribes in 1673, taking the lives of half the warriors.

Stockett's Town continued to prosper under the family's ownership, but after nearly thirty years, the Stocketts sold the property to Dutch fur trader Jacob Looten of Cecil County in 1688. Then, in 1695, Maryland's colonial government made a decision that greatly impacted the small town. The government established a post road to ease the delivery of mail and ran it right through Stockett's Town to the banks of the Susquehanna River.

Two gentlemen, Jacob Young and William York, realized the profit potential that existed in connecting the post road across the Susquehanna River. They set up a ferry in 1695 to connect the road from Stockett's Town on the west coast of the river to Perryville on the east. The ferry they established eventually passed out of their hands but continued to operate for 170 years, transporting both the post (mail) and travelers like George Washington safely across the Susquehanna many times. Because of the ferry, the town earned the name Susquehanna Lower Ferry.

A second ferry, dating to 1727, ran north of Young and York's ferry from present-day Lapidum on the west coast to Port Deposit on the east. It transported citizens wishing to cross the river but did not service the post road. It was known by multiple names through the years, including Smith's Ferry, the Upper Ferry, Bell's Ferry and Creswell's Ferry.

The post road was a very important development for the colonies, and the fact that it ran through Susquehanna Lower Ferry helped the area

A Ferry Scene on the Susquehanna at Wright's Ferry, near Havre de Grace. Although Wright's Ferry is in Pennsylvania, this image illustrates how the ferry transported people and carriages across the river. Watercolor by Pavel Petrovich Svinin, circa 1813. *The Metropolitan Museum of Art.*

tremendously in terms of economic growth and development. Not only did the post road allow news to travel between the colonies, but food and material goods from other locations, and even from England, were able to reach the area. Additionally, taverns and boardinghouses began to spring up to provide food and lodging for those traveling the road.

The post road was also the "information highway" of the colonies and allowed people to receive news from other colonies within a matter of days. An ad in the April 28, 1738 *Virginia Gazette* gives a detailed glimpse at how news traveled during the time period:

> *Alexander Spotswood, Esq., Sole Deputy Post-Master-General of America, having formed a new regulation for carrying on the several Post Stages with greater expedition and certainty than hitherto, this is to advertise the Publik thereof; and that by this regulation the several Stages will be performed as follows, viz: The Post is to set off from the General Post Office at New Post on Wednesdays, the 26th. Inst. To cross over Potowmack that night, and arrive at Annapolis on the Friday: there he is to make some stops and*

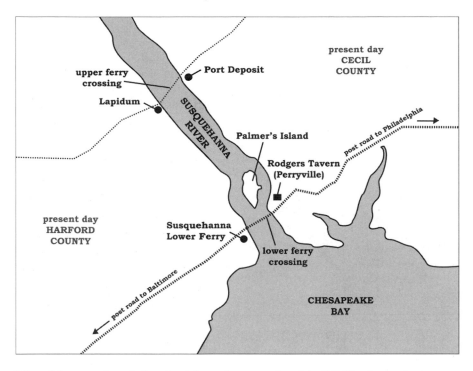

Map of ferry crossings during the eighteenth century, based on C.P. Hauducoeur's map. *Author illustration.*

then proceed to Susquehanna, where he is to arrive on Saturday night; and exchange Mails with the Philadelphia Rider, who is there to meet him; The Monday following he is to return to Annapolis, and arrive at Potowmack on Tuesday night, from whence the Mail is to be brought to New Post on the Wednesday, and the next morning to set out for Williamsburg where he is to arrive on Saturday.[14]

This excerpt is particularly interesting because it cites the rider from Virginia "proceed[ing] to Susquehanna"—or Susquehanna Lower Ferry—to meet the rider from Philadelphia to swap their letters and news items. To think that the exchange of information between the northern and southern colonies was occurring right in Susquehanna Lower Ferry is quite exciting to ponder.

By the 1770s, the post road, which was also known as the King's Highway, was wide enough that stagecoaches could travel reasonably well. Stagecoaches were an early form of public transportation and made trips to the large cities of the time, such as Boston, New York, Philadelphia, Baltimore and Charleston.

Map of the King's Highway.

They consisted of a carriage, usually covered, on which people purchased a ticket to ride from one city to another. The term "stage" refers to the distance of travel—usually about ten or twenty miles—between stops to switch out the team of horses and the driver.

A traveler could take a stagecoach from Boston to Savannah in twenty-four days, and taverns became necessary respites where weary travelers could get a meal and a night's sleep. Locals also frequented their town's taverns, where they could converse with the travelers lodging there. "Newspapers were few and not in general circulation, and the people depended on the gossip of the day for their news, and often on the political harangue for their politics."[15] Taverns became important hubs for the exchange of information.

A tavern bearing the name Stevenson opened in 1740 on the eastern side of the river at the ferry entrance near Perryville and was purchased in 1780 by a Scotsman, Colonel John Rodgers. This tavern played host to famous visitors like James Madison, the Marquis de Lafayette, Thomas Jefferson and George and Martha Washington. In fact, George Washington recorded over thirty stays at Stevenson's and Rodgers's Tavern in his diary, stopping there for a meal and a bed on his frequent trips between his home at Mount

Rodgers's Tavern still stands in Perryville today. *Author's photo.*

Vernon, Virginia, and his not-insignificant commitments up north, including the Continental Congress, the Constitutional Convention, the Revolutionary War and two terms as president.

Stagecoaches were quite plentiful in the late eighteenth century in Susquehanna Lower Ferry. We know this from an entry by Francis Bailey in his *Journal of a Tour in Unsettled Parts of North America, in 1796–1797*: "From Baltimore to Philadelphia are ninety-eight miles; between which places there is no want of conveyance, as there are three or four stages run daily."[16] However, despite the quantity of stages and their usage by luminaries to travel north and south, travel by stagecoach was not luxurious. George Washington complained that he'd had to abandon many a coach after travel through Maryland had "rendered [them] incapable of any further service."[17]

Travelers of the time period made no secret of the terrible condition of the roads. An editorial in the *Maryland Journal* in December 1785 commented on this problem: "It is a truth in which we are all agreed, that all our roads, without an exception, are in the most ruinous condition; that it is extremely difficult, and even dangerous for either carriages or horses to travel on our

Waterloo Inn, the first stage from Baltimore to Washington, 1827. *MDHS.*

most public and frequent roads; and that both our agriculture and commerce are much discouraged by the difficulties and accumulated expences [*sic*] of bringing the produce to market."[18] Another traveler complained that "tree stumps dotted the upland sections of the roadbed while the low-lying stretches, laid out through streams and marshes, were routinely rendered impassable by rain and snow."[19]

Walking the road was no better. "Charles Wilson Peale's journals, for example, relate how he frequently found himself wading through streams with 'mud and mire' over 'the tops of my boots' while traveling the post road through Harford County."[20]

The terrible road conditions, ironically, helped Susquehanna Lower Ferry develop economically. Sometimes travelers would be forced to spend two or three days at the taverns in town while they waited for a storm to pass, tides to lower and roads to dry. The post road, ferries and taverns were responsible for the area's rise in fortune.

Adding to the development of Susquehanna Lower Ferry was John Stokes, who had purchased the land in 1713, and his grandson, Robert Young Stokes, who mapped the town with street names in 1781. In 1785, it was incorporated as a town called Havre de Grace with its own government.

There are several theories on how the area acquired its unique French-sounding name. The town's favored explanation is that the French army

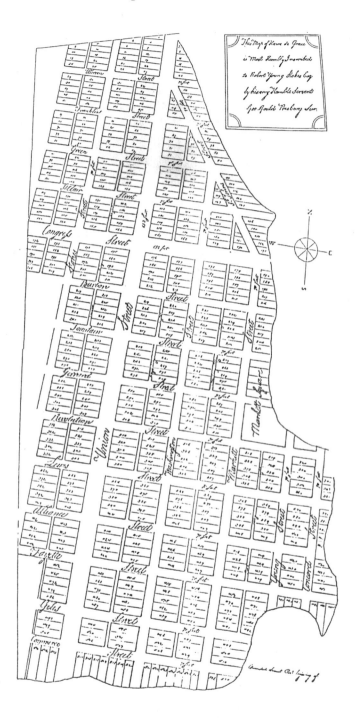

The 1781 map drawn by Robert Young Stokes.

officer the Marquis de Lafayette passed through the area in 1783, after the end of the Revolutionary War. Upon seeing the town nestled along the Susquehanna River and Chesapeake Bay, he exclaimed, "C'est Le Havre," as the landscape reminded him of the French town Le Havre. Legend has it that the name stuck and was made official via incorporation.

Another town legend is that Havre de Grace was only one vote shy of being chosen the nation's capital instead of Washington. This story was debunked by the late historian J. Alexis Shriver. According to Shriver, Havre de Grace was proposed as a location for the capital in 1789, along with two towns in Pennsylvania: York and Wright's Ferry. A specific vote was taken on locating the capital at Havre de Grace, which got a tie vote of twenty-seven people for it and twenty-seven people against. Therefore, the town was dropped from consideration, and Washington was eventually selected. A vote specifically between Havre de Grace and Washington was never formally taken.[21]

Although Havre de Grace did not become the capital of the newly formed nation of the United States of America, it did go on to play an important role in the new country's history.

Nineteenth-Century Life in Havre de Grace

At the turn of the nineteenth century, the people living in Havre de Grace had been citizens of the United States of America for fourteen years. The new nation had been founded on the beliefs of life, liberty and the pursuit of happiness. And the residents of Havre de Grace found their town a perfect spot to pursue happiness.

As John Smith and George Alsop had recorded in their diaries over one hundred years prior, the area's first merit was its splendor and beauty. Its riverside location provided beautiful vistas from every vantage point in town.

Additionally, the area was home to a wide variety of wildlife that the villagers could feast on and trade for other material goods. "Seafood such as fish, crabs, and oysters were plentiful, as well as a variety of birds: ducks, geese, loons, grebe, whistling and trumpeter swans, Canadian geese, blue and snow geese, black ducks, and mallards were evidenced to have lived in the area."[22]

The bears, wolves and deer that Alsop mentions in the 1660s were also still roaming the area in the dawn of the 1800s to provide game meat for the residents. Besides the plentiful wildlife, the area was rich with fertile land. The fields in the area were constantly filled with wheat, maize, tobacco and potatoes.

Havre de Grace residents could also feast on the abundance of wild fruit growing in the area. There are records of fruit-producing trees, including mulberries, crabapples, persimmons and wild plums, and bushes full of blueberries, blackberries, raspberries, elderberries, huckleberries, wild raisins and wild grapes.[23]

The area was also full of trees, which were very valuable to the English. England had been cleared of most of its trees, and the wood American trees provided was a coveted commodity. Logs were used to build ships and dwellings, among other smaller items like furniture and utensils.

An ad appearing in the *Maryland Journal* on September 30, 1785, gives details of the area at the time: "To be sold…Swan-Harbour, commonly called Black-Walnut, containing Five Hundred and Eighty Acres. This valuable tract is…advantageously situated on navigable water. There are about 250 acres in valuable Timber, the Remainder in Meadow and Fields well laid off, adapted to the Growth of Wheat, Tobacco, and Indian Corn."[24]

Also making Havre de Grace ideal was its location a short boat ride away from the third-largest city in America at the time—Baltimore, with a population of 46,555. (New York and Philadelphia were larger.) Baltimore had become an important shipping and grain-milling center.

Town planners and speculators had taken notice of this small waterside town and began to promote its land to buyers. In 1799, Charles P.

This map by Charles P. Hauducoeur was drawn in 1799 as a speculative map for what Havre de Grace could become. The large map is interesting for the detail it provides on the shallow areas of the Bay and the landholdings in areas surrounding Havre de Grace. *MDHS.*

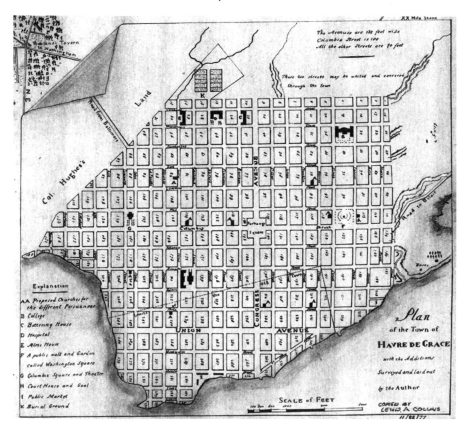

This inset of Havre de Grace on the Hauducoeur map shows the area Stokes had mapped in 1781 and enlarges that area by about three times. The plan included a college, a hospital, an almshouse, a theater, a gaol and a public walk and garden called Washington Square. *MDHS.*

Hauducoeur produced a map of Havre de Grace that "seemed to be a product of an attempt to make it a prominent port and city for the transshipment of freight,"[25] similar to the much larger Philadelphia. On it, he included a theater, town gardens, a hospital, a college and an almshouse, among other institutions.

Minerva Denison Rodgers, whose father bought the Sion Hill property near town and moved to the area in 1801, mentions the Hauducoeur map in her memoirs, saying that "Havre de Grace…had been named as one of the destined places for the seat of government, and I suppose that was one of the reasons that induced my father to purchase land in the vicinity. There had been a French engineer there, who had planned a fine city and had given it the name of Havre de Grace, which it has always retained. I have seen this plan with its fine avenues and streets, churches and theaters, as it was then projected."[26]

Minerva's quote sheds some light on what Hauducoeur envisioned for the town of Havre de Grace but manages to turn two other town myths on their ears. First, she implies that the story of the area becoming a capital city may have had more credence than was discussed previously. Secondly, she states that Hauducoeur named Havre de Grace, not Lafayette.

This is not the place to dissect either claim looking for truth but rather to acknowledge that there are different theories on some key elements of Havre de Grace's history, and the definitive truth might be lost to time. What is not in dispute, however, was the growth Havre de Grace was experiencing, thanks in no small part to the speculative materials being circulated.

By 1803, the area had attracted the notice of architect Benjamin Henry Latrobe, a renowned architect who had designed the U.S. Capitol building in Washington. He wrote to Thomas Jefferson "about the glorious future awaiting Havre de Grace." He predicted that because of Havre de Grace's location on a deep bay, the area would soon rival Philadelphia and Baltimore as a commercial center. "One Million Bricks were laid during the year 1801 in building stores and houses in Havre de Grace and double that number is expected this year," wrote Latrobe to Jefferson.[27]

Thanks to the convergence of the post road, ferries and taverns, there was a daily influx of travelers, and the town was thriving. Merchants were able to set up stores, and the community that once housed small self-sufficient farms gave way to a seaside town with about seventy-four residents, according to the 1810 census. Add the travelers and farmers who lived outside Havre de Grace but made weekly trips into the town for goods, and the merchants could make a living for themselves.

The presence of taverns in Havre de Grace has been well documented, and we can give names to the two main taverns in town during the early nineteenth century: Mrs. Sears's Tavern and Mr. Mansfield's Tavern. It is believed Mrs. Sears's Tavern was located where the American Legion building currently stands (501 St. John Street) and that Mr. Mansfield's stood slightly north of that, with Mr. George Bartol's land in between. The ferry landing was at present-day David Craig Park.

Reverend James Jones Wilmer remarked on the taverns in his first-person account of the attack on Havre de Grace: "The houses (Sears and Mansfield) both were very well kept in every respect, and the traveler found every possible advantage in the competition for both, thereby endeavoring to please, and I verily believe, both were meritorious of their vocation."[28]

It is interesting to note that, although Mrs. Sears and Mr. Mansfield ran the taverns, neither actually owned the building in which they did business. William B. Stokes was Mansfield's proprietor, and Samuel and Tench Ringgold were Sears's.[29]

It is unknown what type of lease Mrs. Sears had with the Ringgolds, but an ad that ran in the *Republican Star* in 1809 indicates it may not have been a long-term one:

> *To be Rented. The subscriber offers to rent that valuable tavern in the town of Havre de Grace, Harford County, Maryland, with the ferry attached thereto, on the western shore of the river Susquehanna, occupied at present by Mrs. Ann Sears. This property is too well known to need a minute description. It is one of the best and most productive stands as a public house in the state, being situated on the main mail road between Baltimore and Philadelphia; the buildings are in every respect capacious and convenient. From a person well acquainted with his business, who has friends sufficient to keep a good house and ferry, and who can give us satisfactory assurances that his deportment to travelers will be obliging in expediting their passage across the ferry at all times, a very moderate rate will be asked. Application for the above property must be made (if by letter, post paid) to Tench Ringgold, Georgetown, Columbia. Possession will be given on the first of October next. Samuel Ringgold, Tench Ringgold.[30]*

We know that Mrs. Sears was still running her tavern during the British attack in 1813, so no better offers must have resulted from the ad.

An ad taken by Mr. Mansfield in the *Federal Republican and Commercial Gazette* in 1810 paints a vivid picture of his operation and hospitality, as well as early nineteenth-century marketing tactics:

> *To the Public. The subscriber again takes the liberty respectfully to inform his friends and the public in general, that he has, at great expense, put the Upper Tavern and Wharf at Havre de Grace in complete repair—Where he is provided every thing necessary to regale and refresh in comfort "The Way-Worn Traveller." He is at present prepared with a good new substantial horse and carriage boat, and a safe moses built boat for the conveyance of passengers, who may prefer it to the larger one, both manned with alert and experienced ferrymen; he also has a second horse-boat on the stocks, which the builder assures him shall be ready for duty in two weeks. Being thus prepared, the*

subscriber tenders his grateful acknowledgements to those who have in the infancy of his establishment, favored him with their calls, and repeats his assurances to the public, that no exertion or attention, by day or by night shall ever be wanting on his part, to contribute comfort and dispatch to all who may please to favor him with their commands… The public's most humble servant, Richard Mansfield, Fountain Inn, Havre de Grace.[31]

Colonel John Rodgers and his wife, Elizabeth, were closely associated with the tavern on the east coast of the river in Perryville that bore their name and the ferry crossing they owned during the late 1700s and early 1800s. Rodgers took over proprietorship of the ferry in 1780, around the same time he purchased the tavern, which still stands today (see photo on page 23). Their tavern was quite popular due to Rodgers's personable nature and the fine menu of "canvas-back duck, shad, and herring from the Susquehanna, and fresh fruits and vegetables grown in abundance on nearby farms in the fertile soil of Cecil and Harford Counties."[32] Dances were also held quite frequently in the building.

Colonel John Rodgers, owner of Rodgers's Tavern and the ferry crossing in Havre de Grace. *Historical Society of Harford County (HSHC).*

The location of a tavern owned by Rodgers on the Havre de Grace side of the river (if there was one) is hazy in today's records. We know that Rodgers and his wife owned a home in Havre de Grace at present-day 226 North Washington Street, a building that still stands today as a retail space.

We have one account of George Washington taking a meal at Rodgers's west side residence, where he recorded: "Thursday, Sept 20, 1787—Set off after an early breakfast, crossed the

Susquehanna and dined at HdG [*sic*] at the house of one (Colonel) Rodgers, and lodged at Skirett's Tavern twelve miles short of Baltimore."[33] Washington dined at Rodgers's Perryville tavern at least thirty times, according to his diaries.

Thanks to the three first-person accounts of the British attack and the 1810 census, we know many of the Havre de Grace citizens during this time. Mr. Kilpatrick and Mr. Burnside were storekeepers who sold groceries and furniture. Mrs. Margaret Miers also had a small grocery. The store Samuel Hoggs & Co. offered clothes, knives and

Elizabeth Rodgers, Colonel John Rodgers's wife. *HSHC.*

forks to its customers, among other material goods. Mr. Christopher Levy and his son William were both hatters, fashioning headwear for both men and women.

Mr. Dunn and Mr. Foreman were both coach makers, an occupation that was very important to a transportation hub like Havre de Grace. Both men kept busy not only building coaches but also making repairs to coaches that had been beaten up by the rough roads and river. "Coaches were strongly built…but they were subjected to a tremendous strain, ploughing [*sic*] through deep mud, plunging into holes, bumping over rocks and stumps, and often they broke down."[34] Mr. John Wareham, the saddler, also benefited in his business of making and repairing horse saddles and bridles for the road's four-legged travelers.

Other citizens included Mr. O'Brien, the schoolmaster; Mr. Dutton, the postmaster; Mr. William Moore, who tended the ferry; and Mr. Mansfield, who, besides managing his tavern, collected the ferry tolls. Town commission records from the time show that various citizens were appointed to serve as inspectors of lumber, flour and salted provisions and as "collector of rents for the streets."[35]

Industries were localized during this time. Mr. John O'Neill owned the nail factory in town, located across the street from his 218 South Washington

Street home, and both Mr. Mark Pringle and Mr. John Stump had warehouses full of flour in town produced from the gristmills they owned.

There was also a significant ironworks on the east side of the river at Principio. This company was owned by Samuel Hughes, who owned a large estate in Havre de Grace (Mount Pleasant) and was one of the wealthy society members of the community.

Fishing was a huge moneymaker for Havre de Grace residents, and small fisheries lined the water's edge. Herring was the most profitable fish breed, but we know that other fish and shellfish were also plentiful along the Bay and river.

When the town was laid out in 1781 by Robert Young Stokes, he decided that Congress Avenue between Market and Washington Streets would be the site of the marketplace. This location was selected because of its ideal situation half a block away from the water and the ferry dock. It was considered *the* center of town, and Congress Avenue was built to be wider along this block to accommodate the extra activity.[36]

The town councilmen decided to finance the construction of a market building, along with St. John's Church (100 North Union Avenue) and its parish house, by a lottery. The total lottery sum of $5,000 was to cover all these structures. The lottery was approved by the state legislature and ran between 1802 and 1807. It appears, however, that the lottery wasn't successful. In 1809, the town commission gave Mr. Mark Pringle and Mr. Samuel Hughes the authority to contract with whomever could help them raise the $5,000 to pay the lottery winners.[37]

Even though the town commission ordered the clerk "to advertise Market Space and the fisheries on adjoining streets for rent" in 1807, it is clear that the commissioners were still scrambling for money to build the market building in 1810. Leftover money from the market building was to go toward a new schoolhouse, which seems a bit ambitious since they hadn't been able to raise the needed $5,000 in eight years' time.[38]

Although it is unclear whether a market building ever was built before the British attack in 1813, the marketplace was still an important space for the community. During this time, public activities of all types were held on the land, including fairs with horse races, music, dancing and food. Militiamen often gathered and trained in the marketplace, and merchants likely still set up booths to sell their wares, building or no building.

The council began construction on its other lottery project, St. John's Church, in 1809, and it is the oldest church in Havre de Grace today. Despite having its own building, the congregation did not have its own preacher at

St. John's Church, from Benson J. Lossing's *Pictorial Field Book of the War of 1812*, 1868.

this time and had to rely on clergymen who traveled from other parishes to Havre de Grace for services.

The records from commission meetings, which were often held at Mrs. Sears's Tavern, provide some quaint anecdotes of life in early nineteenth-century Havre de Grace. In 1803, an act was introduced to prevent geese and swine from roaming the town "at large." In 1809, Mr. Cornelius Chandlee was asked in writing to remove "a nuisance"—stagnant water in his cellar—from his property within one month's time.[39]

In 1812, the citizens were forbidden from "digging or taking away any earth, sand or gravel stones from any of the streets, lanes or alleys, under a penalty of $5," and an ordinance was passed "forbidding the discharge of firearms within the limits of the town." Demonstrating the importance of waterfowl to the economy at that time, it was specified that the ordinance didn't apply to the shooting of ducks or other fowl that were on or over the waters, as long as the shooter was at the water's edge.[40]

Some of the working class of Havre de Grace, such as nail factory owner John O'Neill, could afford small one- or two-room wooden homes. However, most people rented homes from the wealthier landowners in town—Mark Pringle, William B. Stokes (a descendant of John and Robert Young Stokes) and various landlords from Baltimore.[41]

Many alley houses in Havre de Grace were rented as tenement houses, and although none survive in their original state, tax records show there were multiple one-story brick buildings that were two to three bays wide and two rooms deep. The homes were not decorated with any of the architectural embellishments that more wealthy people would have included. It is assumed that many poor working-class people lived in these types of homes.

On the other side of the class spectrum were the wealthy society families of Havre de Grace. The notion of "society" was a holdover from European royalty that implied that these families were more cultivated and educated than the rest of the townspeople. They interacted sometimes exclusively with one another.

The main places in Maryland for society gatherings were Baltimore and Annapolis, and Havre de Grace society did travel to both cities for parties and recreation. But because there were multiple families in Havre de Grace in the upper class, they also socialized at one another's estates, as is illustrated by this quote from Minerva Denison Rodgers, a member of this class:

> *Several wealthy men, tempted* [to the land surrounding Havre de Grace] *by the prospect of its becoming a great city, had bought land and built for themselves very handsome residences. Among them Colonel and Mrs. Hughes, our nearest and most intimate neighbors, and Mr. Pringle, a retired merchant of Baltimore, with his interesting family. In the town of Havre de Grace and just across the river were many pleasant families, which made the society a very agreeable one, especially as they were all hospitable and fond of gaiety.*[42]

The Denison family lived at Sion Hill, one of the great manor homes of the time, where daughter Minerva was single until Colonel Samuel Hughes and his wife invited her and her mother to a dinner party at their estate, Mount Pleasant. It was there that she was introduced to the striking Commodore John Rodgers, whom she married in 1806.

Although Commodore Rodgers was often at sea, the couple made their home at Sion Hill and raised their family there. The mansion sits high on a

Sion Hill, photo taken in 1936. *Library of Congress.*

hill overlooking the town of Havre de Grace, with the front windows facing the Susquehanna River and its chimneys large enough to be seen from boats on the water. The home had formal gardens in the 1800s and today remains one of the leading examples of the Federal architectural style popular during the period.

One of the Rodgerses' neighbors, Samuel Hughes, operated Principio Iron Foundry across the river and had purchased Jacob Giles's Mount Pleasant in 1803. "Local tradition says he 'spared neither money nor labor in beautifying his plantation. It is said Mrs. Hughes had the slaves cut the grass with scissors. They entertained royally."[43] Minerva Rodgers wrote how much she loved to visit Mount Pleasant: "I well remember [Mrs. Hughes's] green and terraced lawns where the first violets and primroses and early spring flowers were to be found. The perfume of the violets and hyacinths still seems to have a power to transport me back to that lovely spot and to the freshness of my early years."[44]

Other estates in the area included Belle Vue Farm, the home of Elijah Davis. He served in both the Maryland House of Delegates and the Senate. His home was likely built in the mid-eighteenth century. Also completed around that same time period was Sophia's Dairy, built by Aquila and

Mount Pleasant as it appeared prior to its extensive 1907 renovation. *HSHC.*

Sophia Hall, and Stafford, the home of the richest man in Harford County, John Stump.

Mark Pringle also had a large mansion, Bloomsbury, in Havre de Grace (near where today's Activity Center is on Lewis Lane). Pringle was a wealthy man with land possessions in both Baltimore and Havre de Grace. Pringle had in his employ in the year prior to the attack on Havre de Grace a tutor named Jared Sparks. Sparks would go on to become the president of Harvard University, but in 1813, he was a twenty-one-year-old student who was taking a year off from college to earn money by working as a tutor for the three Pringle girls, ages ten to fifteen.

In one of Sparks's letters, we get a good picture of Havre de Grace from his eyes:

> *The place at which I now am is a small village, very pleasantly situated at the confluence of the Susquehanna with the Chesapeake. It is a port of entry, and a place of little trade...I find very little similarity between the manners of the people of Maryland and those of New England. That industry and spirit of enterprise, which everywhere prevails in the latter (NE), is*

nowhere to be seen in the former. The farmers here are styled planters. They own vast tracts of land…are gentlemen…never labor themselves, but cultivate their plantations by means of slaves. In short, there are but two classes of people here. The first consists of landholders, who consequently monopolize all the property; the other are tenants, dependents, slaves. The window I am sitting in within half a dozen rods of the Susquehanna, and from it the views of two or three well-cultivated plantations on the opposite shore frequently bring to mind the delightful farms of New England. But when I reflect for a moment that they are made to exhibit this appearance, not by industry and cheerful toil, as in New England, but by oppression and slavery, these pleasing sensations rush instantly from my mind, nor can I endure to dwell on the comparison. [45]

As Sparks makes clear, many landowners used slave labor. We know that Aquila Hall owned slaves at Sophia's Dairy, as did Elijah Davis at Belle Vue and the Rodgers family at Sion Hill. Colonel Samuel Hughes used slaves at both his Mount Pleasant home and at his iron foundry.

Perry Hall, Slave Quarters with Field Hands at Work. Slaves work the land on a plantation in nearby Baltimore County. Oil on canvas by Francis Guy, circa 1805. *MDHS.*

Many slaves tried to escape their life of bondage, not always to good results. A 1798 ad placed by Belle Vue's Elijah Davis in the *Federal Gazette and Baltimore Daily Advertiser* gives us an owner's view on runaway slaves and the lengths he would go to get one back:

> *20 Dollars reward. Ran-away from the subscriber, near Havre de Grace, a negro man, named Bill...about forty years old, five feet ten or eleven inches high; bow legged; broad made; very black complexion; pitted with the small pox; speaks quick. He plays on the fiddle; is fond of boating and very proud. He was seen yesterday in the woods below Abingdon, making towards Baltimore, and was pursued; he may on that account change his route to the Northward. He had on when he was seen below Abingdon a drab great coat, rather short for him, white hat (but took a black one from home) and his hair appeared to be powdered. He had also with him a blue coattee and red jacket. Whoever takes up the above negro and secures him in any gaol, so that the owner may get him again, shall have the above reward, and all reasonable charges paid, if brought home. Elijah Davis, Havre de Grace, December 29.[46]*

Harford County historian Walter Preston summed up slavery in the area this way:

> *Slavery was an established institution, and the masters had that patriarchal manner that comes from the ownership of slaves. The proprietors in the section* [of Harford County] *were, as a rule, kind to their servants, and it was considered bad form to sell a slave. But the institution existing with all its withering effort upon the master and the bondman, and while in the Maryland colony human servitude was found in its least objectionable form, even here its blight only differed in degree from the characteristics in the entire section in which it prevailed.[47]*

However, it is worth noting that Preston wrote this passage in 1901, when views on slavery were much different than they are today, over one hundred years later. The view of patriarchal masters is generally seen as revisionist, and it is impossible to know how the Havre de Grace slave owners actually treated their slaves.

What we do know is that the number of free blacks increased in Harford County during this period. In 1790, there were 775 free blacks and 3,417 slaves (17 percent free), and by 1810, there were 2,221 free and 4,431 enslaved (33 percent free).[48]

So in the years leading up to the War of 1812, Havre de Grace was a fairly prosperous town, home to slaves, farmers, merchants and landowners alike. However, Hauducoeur's plan for a large expansion of the town into a new Philadelphia hadn't panned out. The most pertinent reason for this was because the Susquehanna River was too shallow in the area approaching Havre de Grace and didn't work as a deep-water port. By the 1810s, the town had returned to a small fishing town, still doing business thanks to the post road but not building the colleges and town gardens of Hauducoeur's imagination.

But the happy little town would still be affected by the growing problems the United States government was facing. The townspeople may have been preoccupied with post road travelers and marketplace lotteries, but the newspapers from Baltimore and Philadelphia warned of the growing tensions among the United States, England and France.

WHY WAR?

After winning its independence, the United States continued to grow under the presidencies of George Washington, John Adams and Thomas Jefferson, with the new states of Vermont, Kentucky, Tennessee, Ohio and Louisiana joining the union by the dawn of the War of 1812. During Jefferson's second term from 1805 to 1809, the nation watched as France's Napoleon led his armies in battle across Europe. The United States benefited from trade as a neutral carrier with many of the European nations, including Great Britain and France, and therefore declared itself neutral in the war.

However, as the war intensified, both Great Britain and France ruled that no ships of any country could carry cargo to their opponents without confiscation. While this tactic did little to hurt either warring country financially, it packed a wallop on the American merchant economy, which had been profiting by running supplies to both countries.

As Napoleon squeezed Britain, that country became more desperate for money, goods and men. In response, the British increased their practice of impressment—the forceful pressing of men into naval service. "British law permitted any able-bodied male subject to be drafted into immediate service in the Royal Navy—anytime, anywhere."[49]

This practice resulted in the impressments of more than six thousand Americans into the service of the British Royal Navy and the cargoes of over four hundred American ships seized between 1807 and 1812. "How degrading to a young nation to have its ships stopped, its citizens seized

The impressment of American sailors by the British. *Florida Center for Instructional Technology.*

and then made to serve in virtual imprisonment on board his Majesty's warships," commented one historian.[50]

President Jefferson was frustrated by the actions of both countries and miffed that they were ignoring the rights of his neutral country. "As for France and England," the president growled, "…the one is a den of robbers, the other of pirates."[51]

In the spring of 1807, the British ship *Melampus* anchored at Hampton Roads to wait for two French ships to emerge from the harbor. While it waited, several crew members deserted and promptly enlisted with the United States Navy on the USS *Chesapeake*, which was preparing to sail. When the British demanded their return, Secretary of State James Madison said no, claiming the men in question were actually American citizens. Two were from Maryland: William Ware and John Strahan (or Strachan).

As a result, British naval officials ordered any Royal Navy ship encountering the *Chesapeake* at sea to stop and search it for deserters. HMS *Leopard* tried to fulfill these orders several days later. However, things went wrong when, after trying unsuccessfully to board *Chesapeake* and search its crew, the *Leopard* fired on it, killing three and injuring eighteen. This event, which became known as the "*Chesapeake* Affair," fired the anger of Americans at the British and brought public attention to the problem of impressment.

Upset at this flagrant disregard for America's neutral status, Jefferson passed the 1807 Embargo Act. The act was meant to force both countries to behave; instead, it required a near police state in America to enforce, as many merchants, especially in the northern states, simply ignored the law in order to continue making profits. The act ended up being a disaster for the United States economy and was repealed several days before James Madison was sworn in as president in 1809.

British impressments continued on Madison's watch because the United States didn't have the military might to stand up

President Thomas Jefferson. *Library of Congress.*

to the world's most powerful navy. Although these impressments were happening at sea, far from Havre de Grace, at least one of its neighbors was affected: "A letter has been received by the deputy collector at Norfolk, dated from Liverpool Dec. 8, 1809; written by a James Sparrow, an impressed American, on board the British ship of war *Princess*. He enclosed a list of twenty-five seamen, all impressed like himself: three of 'em are from Maryland: William Frazier, a native of Havre de Grace, Harford County…"[52]

Naval impressments weren't the only problem facing Madison. Other parts of the country were upset with the British and were pressuring the president to act. People living on the western frontier believed that British agents from Canada were instigating the Shawnee Indians, led by Tecumseh, to resist the spread of American settlement. After his tribe was defeated by William Henry Harrison at the Battle of Tippecanoe in November 1811, Tecumseh turned to the British for assistance in fighting the Americans.

TECUMSEH.

Tecumseh. *Library of Congress.*

A March 1812 *Niles' Weekly Register* article captured the feelings on the frontier: "We have had but one opinion as to the cause of the depredations of the Indians, which was, and is, that they are instigated and supported by the British in Canada."[53]

Tecumseh's plan was to form an "Indian confederacy to halt the onslaught of white settlers."[54] His plan was timed properly, as the various states in America were still very self-focused. The North was upset about the shipping embargo and didn't care about the West. The West was upset about the Indian invasions and didn't care about maritime trade. "The people had been brought up as colonists and had been stamped with the characteristics of colonists...Each man concerned himself with his immediate surroundings, which was a colony and was now a state. He was not yet used to his national government, which had taken the place of the European government."[55]

In 1811, the War Hawks were elected to Congress. They were a vocal group of new congressmen from the South and West, and they weren't afraid to let Madison know what he should do. "They called for action, for resistance to Great Britain, for any course that promised to achieve respect for the United States and security for its republican institutions."[56] Madison, who was very intelligent but not skilled in effective leadership, acquiesced and sent Congress a declaration of war on June 1, 1812.

The president's goal was to force Britain to respect the United States' maritime rights. Knowing that he lacked the might of a strong army and navy, he decided the most strategic move would be to invade Canada. Because Canada supplied Britain's Caribbean colonies with supplies, he felt that an attack on its land might effect the desired result.

President James Madison. *Library of Congress.*

Despite this strategic plan for war, Congress believed in a decentralized government and was loath to approve even small appropriations to support the army and navy in America. To support the war effort, Congress ended up appealing to the states and to wealthy citizens for loans.

During 1812, the war focused mainly on the western frontier and the Canadian border. The United States Army was not a match for the well-trained English army. However, the American Navy fared much better.

Captain Isaac Hull and the USS *Constitution* won a significant battle with HMS *Guerriere* on August 19, 1812. The nation rallied around Hull and his ship, which earned the nickname "Old Ironsides" because British shot reportedly bounced right off its sides. Of even more benefit was the $2.5 million Congress authorized after Hull's victory to finance four seventy-four-gun ships of the line and six forty-four-gun frigates.

More victories at sea followed. On October 25, HMS *Macedonian* surrendered to Stephen Decatur of the USS *United States*, and on December 29, the *United States*, this time under the charge of William Bainbridge, defeated HMS *Java*.

To complement its naval ships, the United States began to develop a fleet of privately owned vessels that were able to carry guns in defense of the country. These ships, known as privateers, were granted government licenses called "Letters of Marque" and did a great deal of damage to the British shipping economy by attacking royal merchant ships and taking the cargo for themselves.

The United States government issued 1,100 commissions to privateers between 1812 and 1815. Baltimore led the way in privateering, as shipbuilders there had developed a topsail schooner called a Baltimore clipper, which was extremely fast.

The privateers would come to play a major part in the development of the war as the year turned to 1813. Britain had ended its fight with Napoleon and was able to devote more of its naval resources to the American privateers devastating its trading ships. United States naval ships would continue to play a pivotal role in protecting the United States' shipping interests. It was during this time that the United States Navy became a real power on the seas. And as fate would have it, one of America's most important naval leaders was Havre de Grace's hometown son, John Rodgers.

COMMODORE JOHN RODGERS

Hometown Naval Hero

Commodore John Rodgers, who became one of the most important men in the United States Navy during and after the War of 1812, began life in the waterside town of Havre de Grace. He was born on July 11, 1773, to Colonel John and Elizabeth Rodgers, the owners of Rodgers's Tavern in Perryville and the ferry that crossed the Susquehanna River between that town and Havre de Grace.

John and Elizabeth played a significant role in the growth of Havre de Grace. The future commodore's father came to the area in 1760 from Scotland and was known throughout town as a personable fellow and a shrewd businessman. Upon arriving in the Havre de Grace area, he purchased farmland and gristmills and acted on the moneymaking opportunity the ferry presented by buying Stevenson's Tavern and fashioning it into a welcoming respite for travelers. He also served in the American Revolution after organizing "the fifth Company of Maryland Militia, known as 'The Flying Corps,' which marched north to fight under Washington."[57]

Their son, John, was a typical boy, going to school in the village and playing games with the other boys, serving as the leader in many adventures. He was hardy, strong and enjoyed fowling and fishing along the Susquehanna. It is said he would often swim out in the cold water after dead ducks he had shot from the banks.

Rodgers's Tavern in Perryville. *Cecil County Historical Society (CCHS).*

Young John was also exposed to some great Revolutionary minds in his formative years, thanks to his father's tavern. George Washington was a guest at the tavern many times, and the dinner table was also frequented by the likes of James Madison, Thomas Jefferson and the Marquis de Lafayette. One wonders what knowledge of the world and democracy John absorbed from these gentlemen, who were responsible for the founding of our nation.

Not only did luminaries of the Revolution pass through Havre de Grace, but many lived there as well. The land speculation caused by the Hauducoeur map led many learned, wealthy men to build Federal villa homes on the hills surrounding the Susquehanna River and Chesapeake Bay. The location was not too far from New York, Philadelphia and Washington, and the landed gentlemen of Havre de Grace were all movers and shakers in the political scene. Dr. John Archer, John Adlum, Gabriel Christie, Aquila Hall, William Paca and Robert Smith[58] all lived in the Havre de Grace area, and all were tied to signers of the Declaration of Independence, the Jeffersonian government or both.

But what really fascinated young John were books of sailors and life at sea. He had seen the schooner-rigged ships that docked at Havre de Grace's ports and longed to see a large square-rigged ship. At the young age of thirteen, he took matters into his own hands and set out on foot toward Baltimore, which was thirty-five miles away. His goal: to get a job on one of those ships.

His father, who had followed him to Baltimore, tried convincing him to return home, but Rodgers stubbornly refused. The elder Rodgers decided that if he couldn't get his son to return to the safety of his home, he would at least find him an appropriate apprenticeship aboard a ship. He bound the young John to Baltimore Captain Benjamin Folger, a highly respected shipmaster.

Folger changed ships multiple times while Rodgers was under his tutelage, but they stayed together throughout his apprenticeship, sailing ships owned by Baltimore financiers Samuel and John Smith. Folger was

Secretary of the navy from 1801 to 1809, Robert Smith lived near Havre de Grace and greatly influenced Commodore Rodgers as a mentor and friend. *Navy Art Collection.*

responsible for making Rodgers an excellent sailor. "To Folger, Rodgers was in no small degree indebted for his superior seamanship, his high standards of duty, and his complete mastery of his calling. His steady habits, willingness to accept responsibility, and skill as a sailor soon won for him the favorable opinion of [Folger]."[59]

After making trips to France, the West Indies and Holland with Folger, the Smiths recognized Rodgers's skill and placed him in charge of his own ship, "the 300-ton *Jane*, twice as large as the average Baltimore ship of her day."[60] Rodgers sailed *Jane* throughout Europe and the Caribbean, and his return was announced in the *Federal Gazette and Baltimore Daily Advertiser* at the end of September 1796, about twenty-two months after its departure.

Newspapers, aside from listing the departures and arrivals of ships, were also in the habit of listing what goods had recently arrived from overseas. Therefore, we have a record of the types of items *Jane* was carrying from an ad run by Baltimore merchants Yates and Edmonson: "*Jane* from Liverpool:

an handsome assortment of Fall goods—Consisting of superfine and second cloth, cashimeres, swansdowns, rose and striped blankets, flannels, plaids, bed ticks, checks, stuffs, worsted and yarn hosiery, white and brown linens, velvetrets, thicksets, etc. etc. which they offer for sale on the usual terms."[61]

During Rodgers's first voyage as a captain, only in his early twenties and younger than most of his crew, he drew on his experience swimming in the icy waters of the Susquehanna to prove his grit and mettle. During a 1795 voyage in the frigid North Sea, he lost several sailors who had frozen to death. When he one day ordered his sailors to climb the rigging in the icy cold, they refused. "Outraged, [Rodgers] stripped off his jacket and shirt, wearing only his trousers and shoes...went aloft, telling his crew he would show them what a man could do. Ashamed of their weakness, they soon followed and never afterwards showed a disposition to question his orders."[62]

Longing for greater adventure than commanding a merchant ship, and having proved his skill at sailing the high seas, Rodgers was appointed a second lieutenant in the U.S. Navy on the 1,200-ton frigate *Constellation* in 1798. He quickly moved up the ranks to captain, becoming the first officer in the American navy to be advanced to this rank.

After a stint in jail for aiding one of Napoleon's enemies, he headed back to Havre de Grace in 1802, where he was lauded as a hero for his role in ending the Barbary Wars. In June of that year, Rodgers attended a dinner party hosted by Havre de Grace high society couple Colonel and Mrs. Hughes at Mount Pleasant. Also in attendance at that party was Minerva Denison, a young girl of only seventeen, who was destined to become his wife. Minerva lived in the great house on the hill overlooking the river, Sion Hill.

We get the full story of their meeting and ensuing romance from Minerva's memoirs. On the day of the meeting, her mother had been invited to dine at the Hugheses' home, and it was requested that Minerva attend also. She had not met the captain but said she knew his mother, sisters and one brother and that "he had been much talked of and published in the papers."[63]

Upon arriving at the Hugheses', she sat in the parlor with the other ladies. She tells the story:

> Soon after that the gentlemen came in from the dinner table. I was sitting at one end of a card table which was placed near the wall. Upon the table was a large French clock which effectually concealed any one sitting behind it. Captain Rodgers came in with the quiet determined step...and sat down at the further end of the table from me...While I was sitting at the table

I thought that I would take a peep at the gentleman on the other side of the clock. I bent forward to do so, and to my consternation, I found a pair of piercing black eyes fixed upon me. I withdrew my gaze hastily. The gentlemen all arose and walked into the garden.[64]

After this, Rodgers began to visit Minerva at Sion Hill and made, according to Minerva, "his attentions to me very conspicuous."[65] However, he was then ordered to sea, and their romance paused. He returned to Sion Hill in 1804 to ask her to marry him, and she accepted. After another period of time at sea, during which he was promoted to the highest rank of commodore, Rodgers returned home to marry Minerva in 1806. At the time of their marriage, he was thirty-three to her twenty-two.

Unfortunately no description of the bride has come down to us. We know that she was a most comely and amiable young woman, a blonde with "pretty yellow hair," and rather short in stature…He was a muscular, vigorous man, buoyantly alive, brave and modest, capable of deep feelings and strenuous energy; a little above the average in height, abundant coal-black hair, dark eyes and dark shaggy eyebrows; a handsome face bronzed by seawinds and sunshine, an open countenance as befitted a sailor, and look of firmness and resolution with a touch of imperiousness.[66]

An incident that occurred one day in Havre de Grace demonstrates with clarity the type of man Rodgers was. It was spring, and the ice on the Susquehanna was breaking up. Residents of the town saw what they thought to be an animal trapped on a cake of ice. Rodgers used a spyglass to realize it was a Negro family (or a Negro woman; reports vary) trapped on the ice, which was moving rapidly downstream. A boat was not able to serve in the rescue because of all the ice near shore, so Rodgers took several boards and laid bridges from cake to cake to save the family, while the whole town watched from the shores.

Rodgers's primary reason for being at home in Havre de Grace during this period—aside from spending time with his new wife—was to construct a gunboat for the United States Navy, as ordered by President Thomas Jefferson. Congress had seen fit to reduce the number of servicemen in the navy after the Barbary Wars ended, so Jefferson assigned some of his best commanders to build vessels that "cost but little to build, and almost nothing for maintenance as they could be hauled up on shore safe from the ravages of wind and wave."[67]

Commodore John Rodgers. *National Gallery of Art.*

Rodgers armed his boat, "Gunboat No. 7," with cannon made by his neighbor Colonel Samuel Hughes, owner of Principio Iron Foundry. The end result had "the renown of being counted one of the fastest sailing vessels on our waters—according to Commodore Thomas Tingey."[68]

Hughes was no stranger to equipping navy ships with guns. His Principio Iron Foundry had produced two-thirds of the Model 1794 guns for frigates that fought in the American Revolution, and in 1807, the navy would contract with him for longer twenty-four-pound carriage guns, thirty of which were placed on the USS *Constitution* in 1808.

After Jefferson passed the Embargo Act of 1807, Rodgers received orders to report to New York and take command of the gunboat flotilla stationed there. It was Rodgers's job to enforce the law along the Atlantic coast. While in New York, he and Jefferson also "embarked on a remarkable series of innovative collaborations: they basically invented the concept of dry-docking not-in-use vessels, they established naval bases and other support installations up and down the Atlantic coast, and they revamped the makeup of the fleet, discarding large cumbersome ships in favor of smaller and cheaper gunboats."[69]

On the night of May 16, 1811, Rodgers was aboard his flagship, USS *President*, and saw what he and his crew believed to be HMS *Guerriere* off in the distance. Rodgers gave chase and determined that he was actually in pursuit of HMS *Little Belt*, a much smaller ship. Both ships' captains refused to identify themselves, and shots were fired. Both captains claimed the other fired first, and there is still no real clarity on the issue. However, what is clear is that the *President*'s crew only sustained one injury, while *Little Belt* suffered eleven sailor deaths and twenty-three injuries. The event became known as the "*Little Belt* Affair" and was one of the contributing factors to the War of 1812.

After the war began, Rodgers commanded the *President* for most of the engagement and captured twenty-three British ships. While he was away, he maintained a faithful correspondence with his loving wife, Minerva, who mostly fretted about his safety and wished him home so she could again be happy.

On April 23, 1812, she wrote:

> *I am now writing from Havre de Grace. This place at present presents quite a busy scene in consequence of it being the midst of the fishing season. But I take no interest in anything that is going on, absent from you. I feel solitary and alone. Whenever I look out and contemplate the bustle around me I cannot but think how happy I should be to saunter along the shore hanging on your arm, with Robert [their son] playing his gambols before us.*[70]

A month later, on May 17, 1812, she wrote again:

> *Nothing of any consequence has accured [sic], indeed this place as usual is very barren of incident. I have not been out of the house except to visit your*

mother and once to Mt. Pleasant. We have a new clergyman here but I have not been pious enough to go to church…I am afraid I shall become a very unsocial being for I have little or no relish for society. Nothing affords me any amusement or excite a smile but the innocent endearment and playful gambols of the children.[71]

Havre de Grace's citizens loved and embraced their hometown naval hero. His contemporaries also respected him, with Benjamin Henry Latrobe, the architect who designed the U.S. Capitol building, writing in a letter to his brother: "On the shore, [Rodgers] is a good farmer, a most amiable husband and father, and in all respects unimpeached and unimpeachable morals. He is also the most powerful man in respect to bodily strength in the country and while he could crush us common fellows to atoms, he is peaceful as if he was on a level with us."[72]

THE BRITISH IN THE CHESAPEAKE

As the year 1812 drew to a close, the British had suffered a series of humiliating defeats to the United States Navy, including those at the hands of John Rodgers and his fleet out of New York. Up until then, the action of the war had been contained to the seas and the Canadian border, and Havre de Grace citizens had likely given little thought as to how the war might affect them.

However, the British set their sights on the Chesapeake Bay region in early 1813, a tactic aimed at pulling American troops away from the Canadian front and combating the privateers who were attacking British shipping vessels. When President Madison did not reposition American troops on the eastern seaboard as British officials had hoped, they declared a blockade of the Chesapeake and Delaware Bays as an attack on the $1 million American shipping business being conducted out of Baltimore and Washington.

Although the British plan was aimed at winning the war, the people living in the Chesapeake Bay region were not aware of the big picture. They were aware, however, that there were British ships gathering in the Bay. Rumor in towns lining the water had it that the British "were resolved, for reasons not very distinctly known, to commit depredations on them particularly, and to make them acquainted, not only with the apprehensions, but with some of the realities of war."[73]

British Admiral Sir John Borlase Warren arrived in the Bay in February 1813 to prevent the American privateers and merchant ships from exiting the waterway and to protect British merchant ships from American raids.

He was joined a month later by Rear Admiral George Cockburn, who was placed second in command of the Chesapeake Bay operation.

Cockburn's naval career to this point bore marked similarities to Rodgers's. He became a captain's servant at the young age of ten, having received the placement through his wealthy family's connections. He quickly mastered the seas as Rodgers did and was named a lieutenant by the time he was twenty-one years old. By the time he was forty, Cockburn had reached the flag rank of rear admiral, about five to eight years ahead of the typical age for such a promotion.

Besides the similarities in their career paths, Cockburn and Rodgers both shared a similar rapport with their sailors. British midshipman Robert J. Barrett said that Cockburn was "an officer who never spared himself, either day or night, but shared on every occasion, the same toil, danger, and privation of the [lowliest sailor] on his command."[74]

At the end of 1812, Cockburn was assigned to protect merchant ships near Spain, but his commanding officer soon decided his talents would be better put to use in Britain's war with America. Cockburn was ordered to the Chesapeake Bay to take command of HMSs *Poictiers*, *Victorious* and *Dragon*, his flagship *Marlborough*, seven other minor warships and four frigates, *Maidstone*, *Junon*, *Belvidera* and *Statira*.

His orders for his mission were quite clear, as this excerpt illustrates:

> *To blockade the ports and river harbours in the Bay of Chesapeake and of the River Delaware in the most strict and rigorous manner…*
> *To capture and destroy trade and shipping off Baltimore…*
> *To obtain intelligence of the numbers of gunboats and state of the enemy's ships operating in the Chesapeake and elsewhere.*
> *To procure pilots, taking black men if necessary for all Chesapeake rivers.*[75]

Rear Admiral Cockburn arrived at the entrance to the Chesapeake Bay on March 3, 1813, just two months to the day before his attack on Havre de Grace, and had 180 seamen and 200 Royal Marines placed under his direction. Warren sailed no farther north than Annapolis, leaving the operation in the Upper Bay to Cockburn.

As Cockburn sailed up the Bay, he began orchestrating attacks on the towns lining the Chesapeake. These attacks had two purposes; one was to resupply his sailors with food and supplies. The second, more sinister, purpose was to instill fear and terror in the residents along the Bay. However, British admirals were instructed not to lose sight of their prime objective.

Rear Admiral George Cockburn. *Library of Congress.*

First Secretary of the Admiralty John W. Croker instructed Warren and his men on April 28, 1813: "You must be content with blockading [the Chesapeake Bay's] entrance and sending in occasionally your cruisers for the purpose of harassing and annoyance."[76]

British Captain Frederick Chamier described the nature of the raids: "The more you ruin in a war, the more you hurt the nation at large…the hue and cry always was—'Respect private property, pay for what you take but take care to take all you can' and under this wholesome legislation we burnt and destroyed right and left."[77]

In early April, Cockburn in the *Marlborough*—along with the frigate *Maidstone*, the brigs *Fantome* and *Mohawk* and the three tenders *Dolphin*, *Racer* and *Highflyer*—sailed north up the Chesapeake Bay to penetrate the rivers there. Cockburn took the time to map the waterways and shoals (shallow areas) as he traveled so the British would know the waterways as well as the Americans.

As he sailed near Fort McHenry to map the waters there, his visit caused nervousness among Baltimoreans. Cockburn knew it, ending his April 19 letter to Warren with "I transmit also an intercepted Letter which will give you Some idea of the Effect of our appearance here has had on Baltimore and of the Precautions taken in consequence thereof."[78] The letter he included was from U.S. Captain Charles Gordon to American Secretary of the Navy William Jones, written on April 27. It said: "The alarm increased to such a degree that the Citizens are packing up their valuables, and it is rumour'd the specie [money] will be removed from the Banks."[79] However, Cockburn wasn't yet ready to attack Baltimore, and to the citizens' relief, he only charted the water depths around the fort and turned his fleet north.

Spring was taking hold in the seaside town of Havre de Grace in late April 1813, with farmers tending their fields, fishermen hauling in their nets and stagecoaches making daily runs through town and across the Susquehanna River to Perryville. However, as early as April 20, the residents of Havre de Grace became aware of the British action in the river. Word began to spread around town that the British were advancing up the Bay toward the north, and tongues wagged about whether they were in imminent danger.

"The inhabitants of this place are all in commotion in consequence of the appearance of some British frigates off Turkey Point," Minerva Rodgers wrote to her husband in her letter dated April 22:

> *Many people are alarmed but I do not conceive that there is any danger of their molesting us—there is a gun mounted at any rate which if it will*

Townspeople discuss the movement of British ships in the Chesapeake Bay. *National Park Service/© Gerry Embleton.*

> *consent to go off will give them a warm reception in case they think* [it]
> *proper to pay us a visit. I am not alarmed in the least and if you hear*
> *anything of all this as you probably will with exaggerations be assured*
> *that I am not to be frightened by idle threats, and shall feel myself perfectly*
> *secure at Sion Hill.*[80]

On April 24, 1813, *Niles' Weekly Register* reported: "At Elkton and Frenchtown…the people are well aware of the movements of the enemy. They have thrown up several breastworks and mounted a number of cannon, &c."[81]

On April 28, a few of Cockburn's ships docked in the Bay at Specutia Island, a few miles south of Havre de Grace. They landed at the height of fishing season, which was a busy time on the island. The residents were naturally frightened at first, but the British assured them they would not be harmed. However, guards were stationed around the island to keep the residents from leaving to warn neighboring towns of the British presence.

According to the Reverend James Jones Wilmer, who wrote an 1813 account of the attacks in the Upper Bay, "the officers dined with the tenants [of Specutia Island], some at one house and some at another, and amused themselves with shooting and fishing. I understood they procured some supplies in vegetables, poultry, and roasting pigs for which they made compensation."[82]

Like those in Elkton and Frenchtown, the citizens of Havre de Grace were also making preparations for defense. Jared Sparks was residing in the town at this time as the tutor of the Pringle children and several years later published an account of the attacks in the region. His account states:

> *The inhabitants of Havre de Grace had, for three week previous, been making preparations for defence* [sic] *and several companies of militia were called in to their aid...A battery was thrown up at Point Concord, where the river unites with the bay, behind which were mounted an eighteen-pounder and two nines. These were manned by a company of volunteers, principally exempt from military service.*[83]

The town was mainly being protected by volunteers exempt from service, as Sparks stated, because all men of military age were dispatched as members of their units to other parts of the war. Although some cavalry and infantry were assigned to Havre de Grace at the first appearance of the British in the area, they were a disorderly group with absent officers, and Sparks did not feel they took the possibility of an attack on Havre de Grace seriously.[84]

Cockburn made his first offensive move in the early hours of April 29, when he and his men set sail up the Elk River to the east of Havre

Rough sketch of Frenchtown on the Elk River. Benjamin Henry Latrobe, 1806.

de Grace. Their target was a store of government supplies in Frenchtown. Unfortunately for the British, they got lost, and by the time they arrived, they had lost the element of surprise.

The British naval brigade under Lieutenant George Augustus Westphal landed at Frenchtown around eight o'clock in the morning and was welcomed by a six-gun battery. The Americans were no match for the British forces, however, and quickly fled.

A letter that was printed in the *Baltimore Patriot* on May 1, 1813, gives us a clear description of exactly what happened at Frenchtown:

> *I now undertake to inform you of the British arriving here yesterday morning about 8 o'clock. But 5 or 6 barges were at first seen; in a few minutes the river appeared full of them—the whole number was 12 large barges. There had been a battery commenced on the lower wharf, but was not near completed; 4 guns were mounted…A few individuals (eight or ten) manned the guns, and commenced firing when the barges were about a mile off.*[85]

The account goes on to say that the battery expended all of its ammunition before the British barges were a half mile from land, and its efforts did not result in any injury to the enemy. Around the time the battery ran out of gunshot, the British barges began to fire and continued as the four hundred marines landed onshore. Cockburn and his troops fanned out and set fire to the military stores, merchandise and five vessels while disabling the guns in the battery.

In preparation for the Royal Navy's arrival, Frenchtown residents had emptied most of the goods from their lower storehouse; however, there were still 1,500 bushels of oats in the building when the British set it ablaze. The fish house and several fishing boats were also set on fire, as was the second storehouse, which was housing the goods the townspeople had moved out of the lower storehouse.

The gentleman who wrote the account of the Frenchtown attack said that the officers were "exceedingly polite" and did not harm any of the dwellings or personal belongings of the townspeople.[86] One British officer reported that he had been given orders to burn both the stables and the stages at Frenchtown, but neither was actually harmed. Nevertheless, the *Baltimore Patriot* reported that the town itself lost a great amount: "We learn from Frenchtown that the goods in the stores destroyed by the British were about 12 waggon [*sic*] loads, consisting of three loads of copperas, 30 bales of flannels, 5 hogsheads of military clothing, 30 cases of books, containing a number of bibles and prayer

Elkton is shown with three earthwork forts as its battery. *National Park Service/© Gerry Embleton.*

books, and several packages of merchandise."[87] In total, the losses added up to about $30,000 in government equipment and supplies.

Along with the news of the loss at Frenchtown, the May 1 *Baltimore Patriot* also contained a warning. It reported that the British "said they would come up this night with a stronger force to Elkton, and if any resistance was made, would destroy every house in the town. Whether this threat was only to keep the citizens in constant alarm, or if they plan to put it into execution, no one can say."[88]

Burning Elkton would be a solid strategic move for the British, as it was a major center of transportation. Many travelers sailed up the Bay to the Elk River and disembarked at Elkton, where they boarded a stagecoach to Philadelphia. "Well aware that they would be a British target, two hundred Elkton residents met and pledged $1,000 for the construction of three earthen forts and placement of a large chain across the river."[89] This work was completed prior to the attack at Frenchtown.

The British did row up the Elk River toward Elkton after they finished in Frenchtown but encountered defensive fire from two earthen forts, Defiance

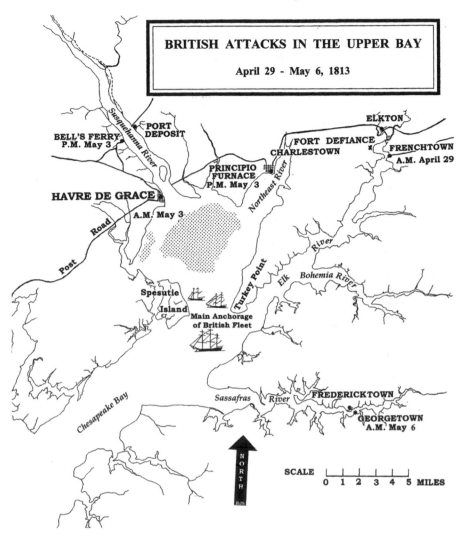

A map of the British activity in the Upper Bay. *Image courtesy Christopher George. Illustrated by Richard Sherrill.*

and Frederick. The chain Elkton had placed across the river prevented their movement farther north, and they quickly turned back and headed for Specutia Island.

It was during this sail that the citizens of Havre de Grace did two things that, unbeknownst to them at the time, sealed their fate. As Cockburn described in his May 3 letter to Admiral Warren, "I observed Guns fired and American Colours hoisted at a Battery lately erected at Havre-de-grace [*sic*] at the entrance of the Susquehanna River, this of course immediately gave to the Place an Importance which I had not before attached to it, and I therefore determined on attacking it."[90] If Cockburn is to be believed, he was not planning on attacking Havre de Grace at all until they fired upon his ships as they returned from Elkton. This seems unlikely, since he had already attacked so many other towns in the Bay.

The American version of the firing is, as expected, different. Wilmer narrates the Havre de Grace side of the story:

> *The cartel which came to Havre de Grace a few days previous to the attack, with prisoners on parole, was not fired on, as has been falsely circulated. On their approach to the battery, Lieutenant Goldsborough ordered the sentry to fire a musket in the air, to let the vessel know that the place was in a state of war…But not the smallest intention of injury was intended or offered.*[91]

This story seems dubious at best. If the citizens of Havre de Grace knew the British were attacking neighboring towns, firing a shot at their passing boat seems foolish. But each story has two sides, and the truth likely lies somewhere in the middle.

British Sir James Scott also felt it was misguided of Havre de Grace to have fired a shot, as he described in his *Recollections of a Naval Life*:

> *The Americans, who had lately erected a battery at Havre de Grace, commenced firing their guns, and hoisted the American colours, by way of bravado; or, which is more likely, thought they should, by such a silly display of their means to annoy, deter the Admiral from making any attempt against them. In the latter case, they woefully deceived themselves, for it immediately attracted his attention, and determined him to attack the place;—if it was worth erecting defences for its security, it was worth an attack.*[92]

It wasn't only the residents of the area who were watching the British movements closely. On May 2, two Philadelphians traveling the post road by stagecoach, Daniel Mallory and his wife, were approaching the Perryville ferry crossing from the north and heard about the burning of Frenchtown. The occupants of the coach discussed whether to alter their course due to the British presence in the area and decided to continue as planned. Mallory related, "As we approached the river, the scene became exceedingly animated and interesting. A few miles south of us were to be seen in full view the enemy's fleet, riding in all the dignity and majesty of triumph, commanded by Admiral Cockburn; the tall masts towering above the forest trees that nearly surrounded the noble looking ships."[93]

After crossing the river to Havre de Grace, the Mallorys and their fellow travelers took lodging at Mrs. Sears's Tavern. Although the party wanted to continue on the post road that night and lodge away from Havre de Grace at Bush, the stage driver did not. We do not know why; perhaps from exhaustion, perhaps from the lack of a perceived threat.

By this time, Havre de Grace's state of alert had slackened. Originally on high alert, their "vigilance continued till [*sic*] within three or four days of the time, when they were actually attacked," explained Sparks.

> *At this time, the inhabitants, wearied with continual excitement and laborious exercise, began to relax from their exertion, and as the English had continued tranquil for some time, without discovering any hostile intentions, they fancied themselves in less danger than they had apprehended. By some unaccountable want of foresight, all the cavalry and some of the infantry were suffered to return to their homes, and those which remained became uneasy and disorderly.*[94]

Mallory confirms a lack of decorum from the militia when he encountered them at the tavern that evening, "dressed out in all the gaudy trappings of a full parade day, to defend by their prowess the domestic altars and firesides of their neighbours of Havre de Grace. They had a late dinner…and from appearances…had indulged pretty freely in the wine cup, or some other exciting beverage."[95] He continues, saying that one man hoped "that [the British] would attempt a landing; he would sink all the boats of the fleet, should they have the temerity to approach his battery!"[96]

It is true that the first days of May passed without incident. The military had been on duty for consecutive nights and was obviously having fun mocking the British, who had parked their ships downriver and were just sitting there. The citizens of Havre de Grace may have thought themselves safe. But, as we know, they were not.

THE ATTACK ON
HAVRE DE GRACE

O n the morning of May 3, 1813, the townspeople of Havre de Grace were sleeping peacefully in their beds. Although British boats had been seen floating near the town's shores, they hadn't created any trouble for Havre de Grace, and the attack they had been warned of had not materialized. There were several men on watch, but the town was feeling relatively—if perhaps naïvely—safe. This is what Admiral Cockburn was counting on when he launched his attack in the early hours of the morning.

Due to his surveillance of the water depths in the area, Cockburn knew he would not be able to get close enough to Havre de Grace's shores to land his large ships. He therefore ordered about 150 men into rowboats under Westphal's command. They rowed the eight miles from Specutia Island toward the sleeping village "to take up under cover of the Night the necessary Positions for Commencing the Attack at dawn of day," as Cockburn reported to Warren after the event.[97] He also sent his tenders the *Dolphin* and *Highflyer* to support the rowboats, but these larger ships could not get closer than six miles to land.

Mr. Boyd, a Havre de Grace resident, lived down near the southern end of the town, closest to Specutia Island, and was the first to notice the advancing British boats. Boyd related the story to Reverend James Jones Wilmer: "As soon as day was advancing the boats got under way and proceeded a little upwards towards the battery…then appeared about sixteen in number, and made their landing at the Point, the four first boats continuing up the river."[98] (Wilmer was one of three men who wrote first-person accounts of the attack; the others are Jared Sparks and Daniel Mallory.)[99]

Boyd references the "battery," which was a fortification where there were three cannon: a six-pounder and two nine-pounders. Unfortunately for historians studying the Havre de Grace attack, neither he, nor Wilmer, nor the other men who wrote first-person accounts was specific about the location of this battery. As a result, there is a good deal of debate among scholars on where precisely this battery was located. For the purposes of this text, we will use Mr. Boyd's account, as retold by Wilmer.[100]

It is likely that some British troops came ashore at Concord Point, where the lighthouse now stands; other boats rowed "upwards towards the battery" and came ashore there, upriver from Concord Point but at the south end of the town. More boats continued farther upriver and landed at the ferry landing near Mrs. Sears's and Mr. Mansfield's taverns at the north end of town.

As the rowboats approached land, the British scared the residents out of their beds with hissing and exploding Congreve rockets, cannon fire and musket shots. Daniel Mallory was staying at Mrs. Sears's Tavern on the night of the attack and told of his frightening experience:

> *Just as the day dawned I was awakened by the report of heavy artillery. It neared with fearful rapidity. I had scarcely time to realize what it was, and our critical situation, when we were startled with a loud report in our room, accompanied with pieces of the wall flying in all directions! This was followed quickly with continuous showers of grape shot, some entering through the upper part of the windows, cutting away the plaster over our heads, while others lodged in the roof...As the firing increased, our situation became more and more irksome and alarming; to add to the horrors of it, I found, on trying to escape, that some one had fastened the door on the outside! I hallooed at the top of my voice for assistance. No response came, All were alive to their own danger and were exerting themselves to the uttermost to flee to a place of safety. The noise and confusion below stairs increased to a painful degree.*[101]

Mallory was subsequently freed from his room by a gentleman passing down the hall.

Mallory, Wilmer (who was also a guest at Mrs. Sears's Tavern that night) and the rest of the townspeople took off running for the hills to the west of town. "The scene that presented itself was animated and picturesque beyond my ability to describe. The air seemed alive with Congreve rockets, squirming and hissing about like so many fiery serpents."[102]

The British fire a Congreve rocket from a rocket boat. *NASA*.

As the people of Havre de Grace fled their homes, they were joined by the majority of the militiamen who had just the night before been boasting of their prowess. However, several militiamen proved their bravery by running to the battery to fire shots back at the British. John O'Neill, one of the heroes in the battery that morning, had the following to say:

> *We had a small breastwork erected with two six- and one nine-pounder in it, and I was stationed at one of the guns. When the alarm was given I ran to the battery and found but one man there, and two or three came afterwards. After firing a few shots the other men retreated and left me alone in the battery. The grape shot flew very thick about me. I loaded the gun myself without anyone to serve the vent, which, you know, is very dangerous, and fired her, when she recoiled and ran over my thigh.*[103]

At this point, O'Neill also fled from the battery, nursing his wounded leg, and set off to join his comrades at the nail factory he owned closer to town.

British Captain Marmaduke Wybourn of the Royal Marines recalled that the "Americans were quickly driven from their guns, having not the courage to await our attack though perhaps the circumstances of a Congreve rocket having been well directed at the outset put them in confusion. It passed through the Battery and struck a man in the back."[104]

A Congreve rocket did strike a Mr. Webster in the back and killed him instantly. This is certainly one reason the men abandoned the battery in such haste. Congreve rockets were developed as instruments of "shock and awe" and were used extensively in the Upper Bay Campaign by the British. They were mostly good for firing into towns to set them on fire, but rarely did they kill people. Poor Mr. Webster, in the wrong place at the wrong time, was hit directly by the weapon and was one of only three fatalities during the War of 1812 by Congreve rocket.[105]

Seeing that the Americans had abandoned their battery, British Captain Lawrence ordered his men off their rowboats and to the battery, where they turned the town's guns inward facing the town and fired them. By this point, O'Neill had joined Mr. Bennet Barnes, Christopher Levy, his son William and John M'Kinney on the marketplace common, where they continued to fire on the British with muskets while trying to summon the frightened militia to return and fight. "They proved cowardly and would not come back," O'Neill succinctly states.[106]

But O'Neill soon faced bigger problems. He was approached by an English officer on horseback who made him a prisoner and carried him aboard the British *Maidstone* frigate, along with five other men, including the elder Mr. Levy and Mrs. Sears's eldest son, James. British Lieutenant Westphal was instrumental in rounding up these prisoners, but one of the Americans—possibly O'Neill himself—succeeded in shooting a hole in Westphal's palm in the process, "much to the amusement of the officer and the men under his command."[107]

Meanwhile, the townspeople of Havre de Grace were running full tilt toward the north and west. "The hills were covered with flying, frightened, and half-dressed people, many of them curiously encumbered with useless and worthless articles, which they had, in their alarm, unconsciously brought away," Mr. Mallory related.[108]

Rear Admiral Cockburn and his men were now on land, systematically setting buildings ablaze that the Congreve rockets had missed. According to Cockburn's report to Warren after the attack, he set "fire to some of the Houses to cause the Proprietors (who had deserted them and formed Part of the Militia who had fled to the Woods) to understand and feel what they were liable to bring upon themselves by building Batteries and acting towards us with so much useless Rancor."[109]

By this time, Wilmer had reached a hill a distance from town:

> *I did see from the heights, the British drawn up contiguous to the Church, supposed to be about 150 in number. I heard the drum distinctly beat, and saw from the reflection of the sun, the glittering of their arms. From hence, they discharged some rockets and sent out small parties with prepared combustibles to fire the town. The first step was plunder without distinction, the next conflagration without delay.*[110]

Sparks further detailed the method of plunder and burning: "Their manner was, on entering a house, to plunder it of such articles as could be of any service to them, and easily transported, and convey them to the barges."[111] This is how the beautiful new carriage that coach-maker Mr.

Admiral Cockburn Burning and Plundering Havre de Grace. Notice the stolen coach out on one of the British boats. British troops plunder baby cradles and dressers. The injured Westphal stands in front of Mrs. Sears's burning tavern on the left, and Admiral Cockburn stands in the middle with a sword. Lithograph by William Charles, 1813. *MDHS.*

Dunn had specially designed for Mr. John Stump was carried off and placed on a British barge as a "present to the lady of Admiral Warren."[112]

Some people remained in town, determined to do what they could to protect their property. Mr. Mansfield was one of these men and reported that he and his son watched the British row up to shore from the tavern with a spyglass. Upon landing, the British moved up to his wharf, examined his ferry for any goods worth stealing and then set the boat adrift. Lieutenant Westphal and his men then arrived at Mansfield's to set the house on fire. No amount of begging from Mansfield was able to save the place or the items inside. Westphal "gave his orders to…instantly fire the house, which they soon did by breaking open the bar door, and destroying bottles containing liquor, throwing the contents onto the floor and then setting fire to the window curtains…thereby communicated to the liquor on the floor, which, in a very short time, set that part of the house ablaze."[113]

When Westphal finally told Mansfield to save what he could, the American ran upstairs to begin throwing furniture and mattresses out the windows. However, the British waiting in his yard immediately carried away the furniture to their ships and ripped the beds to shreds, leaving feathers floating in the air.[114]

Mrs. Sears's Tavern was also destroyed by fire, along with the stables and the ferries. Her neighbor George Bartol lost his grocery store, and Mr. Wareham, the saddler, and Mr. Tucker, the carpenter, lost all their tools, as well as their homes. Captain Lawrence and a few other officers removed several boxes of dried goods from Mrs. Sears's Tavern and the Samuel Hoggs & Co. store. Taking forks, knives, clothing and money as they found it, Lawrence is said to have shouted, "Boys! Here is a fine plunder!" while Mr. Kilpatrick and three other Havre de Grace citizens watched in horror.[115]

Mr. Stokes "was a considerable loser" who lost his home and the furniture in it, as well as a variety of other properties he owned around town, including Mansfield's Tavern.[116]

Gabriel Christie's home, one of the first homes built by one of the first settlers in town, was also ruined. It appears the townspeople were using this place as the magazine, and the British stole all the ammunition and weapons stored there.[117]

The British likely knew Havre de Grace was the hometown of American naval hero Commodore John Rodgers, although Cockburn does not specifically mention the fact in his records. Nevertheless, the enemy set fire to Mrs. Rodgers's home three separate times—this being the home of the commodore's mother, Elizabeth, who had her daughter and son-in-law, Mr.

Elizabeth Rodgers's home, from Benson J. Lossing's *Pictorial Field Book of the War of 1812*, 1868.

and Mrs. Goldsborough, living with her in town. Mr. Goldsborough had evacuated the women out of town to Mr. Pringle's mansion, where many of the townspeople had retreated, but he returned to extinguish the flames at Mrs. Rodgers's, allowing it to survive and stand even today (see photo on page 111). However, a significant amount of furniture and clothing was defaced and stolen from the property.[118]

The family suffered additional losses. Alexander Rodgers, brother to the commodore, lost his store to the flames, and the Goldsboroughs had furniture stored at his place for their new home that was also lost.[119] To make matters worse, the home the Goldsboroughs had just bought (now known as the Aveilhe-Goldsborough House) had a cannonball launched through its front wall and was set ablaze. Mr. Goldsborough was able to extinguish the flames at this home, and it still stands today (see photo on page 112).

Sion Hill, the family seat of Commodore John Rodgers, was too far west for the British to reach, and it suffered no damage from the attack.

The British showed no mercy for even the less fortunate in town. They entered the home of a woman who had just given birth and was unable to leave as the British ordered. They picked her and her infant up by the four corners of her mattress, moved her to another home and set the home she had been in on fire. They also burned "The Company's Buildings," a row of homes principally inhabited by poor people.[120]

Mr. Cornelius McCaskey—a poor man, according to Wilmer—suffered great destruction at the hands of the British:

> *The enemy stripped him of everything that was portable. His clothing and bedding, broke tables and glasses, and mutilated what they did not take away; bore off two guns, many of his tools, and all his wife's clothing. They left him not a knife or fork, and he plead hard for one old knife, which after breaking the handle, they threw at him; which so exasperated the old man that he jumped to his hatchet and was determined to kill the fellow.*[121]

Other British officers interfered and kept this from happening. "There is a spirit in man, at time, above the fears of death and every consideration; and this was the state of this poor old man, driven to destraction [*sic*] by the ferocious banditti."[122]

St. John's Church, the dwelling the town had built with lottery money, also fell victim to the British. Wilmer, a reverend by trade, seemed to believe the British would spare the church, since it was "The English Church" and named after their country. But the British did not see it from that point of view. "Plunder and devastation was the order of the day, and like faithful militants, they were determined not to part from the order at least in doing evil."[123] Thankfully, the British didn't torch the church. They broke all of the windows and damaged the pews and altar, but the church did not burn and still stands in Havre de Grace today with an active congregation (see photo on page 113). This church counted among its nineteenth-century congregation the families of O'Neill, Rodgers and Stump.

Merchants were also made to suffer. Mr. Kilpatrick and Mr. Burnside's store was mutilated; they were robbed and plundered, although the building wasn't burned. Wilmer sums up their affairs well, saying:

> *Thus at one blow, two worthy men have experienced a reverse of fortune, so as to defeat all their fair hopes, and may eventually change their stand and plan of business. The destroying angel came as a thief in the night, with the bosom of destruction; the ministers of wrath had no pity; for*

merit of the afflictions of their fellow-men, but like fiends, as they were, indiscriminately involved all in one common state of ruin.[124]

Wilmer provides an extensive list of other townspeople, what they lost in the attack and an estimated amount of loss, for a total of over $50,000 (approximately $800,000 today). This number includes all the goods that were stolen by the British, as well as losses to fire.

The Reverend Wilmer surely felt for his friends in Havre de Grace as he stood on the heights above Havre de Grace that morning watching it burn. At that moment, all he could see was smoke; it wasn't until several days later that he returned to town to see what had survived in order to write his account.

Mallory provides a vivid picture of the destruction as seen from a distance as he and his wife made their way north to the safety of Colonel Hughes's home, Mount Pleasant: "Behind us the flames and smoke of the burning village, as they circled and rolled about, forming dark thick clouds, which expanded as they were wafted onward by the breeze into various fantastic shapes."[125]

The families who had fled their homes congregated at either Colonel Hughes's or Mr. Pringle's homes, believing they were far enough west not to be torched. However, this was not the case. Many of the people who had sought sanctuary at Colonel Hughes's immediately had to take off running again when word spread that the British had asked for him by name. This turns out to be true—the British did ask where Hughes lived because they knew his iron foundry supplied the navy's weapons. However, upon learning the location of his home, they decided it was too far away and did not pursue it further. His iron foundry would not be as fortunate.

Mr. Pringle had already lost his waterfront warehouses full of flour to the tune of $5,000 when the British showed up at his newly constructed home. However, Mr. Pringle was able to save his residence by meeting the British in his yard "with a white cloth hung off a staff, [begging] them to spare the women and children who had sought shelter with him. They suffered the house to stand."[126]

By this time, "the firing of cannon had ceased," Sparks reported, "and no other noise was heard, than the roaring flames, the crash of falling timbers, and the occasional lamentations and entreaties of a few of the inhabitants, who had braved every danger with the hope of preserving from destruction their only means of subsistence." Two or three of these ladies approached Cockburn and "endeavored by all the powers of female eloquence to dissuade him from his rash purposes. He was unmoved at first; but when they represented to him the misery he was causing, and pointed to the smoking

Pringle Mansion, also called Bloomsbury, from Benson J. Lossing's *Pictorial Field Book of the War of 1812*, 1868.

ruins under which was buried all that could keep their proprietors from want and wretchedness, he relented and countermanded his original orders."[127]

After ensuring the town's destruction, Cockburn sent a detachment of troops north to Bell's Ferry (present-day Lapidum). The townspeople had already heard about the terror in Havre de Grace and were understandably scared. Upon making landfall, the British proceeded to the warehouse of gristmill owner John Stump.

> *They entered it and rolled out a barrel of whiskey, broke in the head, drank what they desired, and then set fire to the building, which was completely destroyed. They also fired a vessel belonging to Mr. Stump, which was riding at anchor near by, which burned to the water's edge. They were then ready to burn the tavern and store house, but desisted upon the entreaties of William Johnson and others who were present. They then took their departure, without committing other depredations.*[128]

Cockburn also had Creswell's Ferry (present-day Port Deposit) in his sights. However, the citizens of that town had built an improvised gun battery that was visible from the river. This was enough of a deterrent to keep the British from venturing into that particular town.[129]

While one detachment was upriver attacking Bell's Ferry, Cockburn took some of his marines and sailed up the Northeast River to continue his busy day terrorizing the Upper Bay. This time, Cockburn intended to hit Samuel Hughes and the American navy where it hurt—the Principio Iron Foundry that was responsible for churning out the cannon on board most of the American navy's ships. The foundry was several miles north of Havre de Grace.

In his letter to Warren, Cockburn stated he learned of the foundry while in Havre de Grace, possibly during his inquiries as to the location of Samuel Hughes's residence. He further says they had no trouble finding or overtaking the foundry and spent the rest of the day destroying the guns, machinery and other materials on site. "It…was one of the most valuable Works of the Kind in America, the Destruction of it therefore at this moment will I trust prove of much national Importance," he boasted.[130]

It is hard to put a price tag on the loss Hughes suffered that day. Although his house still stood, he had lost his business, which was worth thousands. One machine that he used for boring holes in the guns was worth $20,000 on its own. The British destroyed "five 24-pound cannons in a battery meant to protect the ironworks, twenty-eight 32-pounders ready to be shipped, along with eight other cannons and four carronades of different calibers, for a total of 46 cannons destroyed."[131] Plus, the American war effort lost one of its top gun manufacturers.

The ravaging of Principio was the last act of terror for the British on May 3, and the fleet returned back to Specutia Island at 10:00 p.m. Cockburn reported to Warren that they had been "in constant exertion" for twenty-two hours without any nourishment.[132] Surely they were tired and hungry, but their exhaustion was nothing compared to the mental anguish the townspeople of Havre de Grace were facing that night.

Sparks concludes his account:

> *The most distressing part of the scene was at the close of the day, when those, who had fled in the morning, returned to witness the desolation of their homes, and the ruin of all their possessions. Most of them had escaped without being able to take any thing away, except the clothes which covered them. They returned wretched and disconsolate, and seemed overwhelmed*

with the thoughts of misery and want which awaited them. But their immediate necessities were relieved by the benevolence and liberality of a few gentlemen in the neighborhood, who received them kindly into their houses and supplied them with provisions.[133]

And while they may have been mildly consoled that only one townsperson was killed, several families were still missing members—as they were still being held prisoner on the British ship *Maidstone*.

REACTION AND AFTERMATH

D ear Sir—The scene is closed. The enemy took this place this morning, and burnt it. Every house has suffered more or less—mine and all my furniture is gone. I am ruined. My ferry boats are all taken and two stages burnt—all my stables, &c."[134]

This short but powerful statement was published in the *Baltimore Patriot* on May 4, 1813. Although the nineteenth century was in no way similar to the twenty-first in terms of timely coverage of breaking news, it is apparent that the news of the Havre de Grace attack reached Baltimore very quickly. Another entry from the same issue explains why: "By several passengers in the stage which arrived last evening, information is received that about the dawn of day yesterday morning, a considerable number of the enemy came up as high as Havre de Grace, and commenced the bombardment of that place with shot, shell, and rockets. It lasted about 15 minutes. The destruction was general; even the baggage of the stage passengers was destroyed."[135]

Being a newspaper, however, it also had practical matters to address: "As the stages were destroyed and a part of the enemy remained at Havre de Grace, it is probable that no mail will arrive from the north this morning."[136]

The attack on Havre de Grace, which followed on the heels of the attack on Frenchtown, was very jarring news for the citizens of Baltimore. They had been watching the British ships in the Chesapeake Bay for the past few months and were concerned about their own fortunes. The reports appearing in the *Patriot* surely did nothing to calm their nerves: "Another letter of the same date says 'Every house in the town is injured more or less; the enemy after ransacking the place, embarked immediately, and took off nearly all the ferry boats. They commenced the attack at 4 o'clock AM on the 3d inst. With 19 barges, supposed to be manned with 30 to 40 men each, every barge had its object, as all the houses were fired into at the same time.'"[137]

The paper also published this interesting exchange on May 4. It is impossible to know whether this is a transcript of an actual conversation or a type of editorial, but it pointed out to readers in Baltimore how the attack on Havre de Grace could affect them:

Dialogue Between two citizens.

1ˢᵗ Cit: Good morning sir—what's the news?

2d Cit: Nothing of consequence—Do you learn any of the particulars of the destruction of Havre de Grace?

1ˢᵗ cit: No—none of the particulars—tho' it is now reduced to a certainty, that every house in the place was more or less injured.

2d cit: Yes! So I hear—We shall have a visit next.

1ˢᵗ cit: Pshaw! You don't think so—they would never dare to hazard a landing here—and our fort will afford a sufficient defence [sic] against any vessel which can be brought against us.

2ⁿᵈ cit: It is that very mode of reasoning, my friend, which may prove our destruction. We are too confident in numbers, and place too much reliance on inanimate things. The fort, to be sure, if properly manned, will avail much—but can they affect a landing in no other way than by a direct passage of the fort? And are we sure that our very numbers would not prove detrimental, from the confusion that would inevitably ensue in the city, in the present state of things? Has every individual arms in his house? Does every man know where to repair? Is every man drilled and under a proper officer? And are preparations made for the security of the women and the children?

1ˢᵗ cit: Your questions have weight—but with their present force, to imagine them bent on such a project, is to be as ridiculous as they would appear in the attempt.

2d cit: I agree with you, that with their present force, no attempt may be made, but the probability that they will be strengthened, should open every man's eyes to the danger and induce the proper authorities to look about them. Good day.[138]

This passage was surely published by the newspaper editors as a warning to Baltimoreans not to get too complacent. It also served as a call to the public to make the necessary preparations for a potential attack and was likely also directed at the government to ready the militia and fortifications.

Additional commentary addressing the government and the public was included in this passage from the same *Patriot* issue:

> *To the citizens of Baltimore. One of the towns in your vicinity has been sacrificed to British vengeance. We see in the smoking pile of Havre de Grace, what we ourselves have to apprehend, when they shall have accomplished the concentration of a force, sufficiently great to authorize an attempt on this "devoted city." The news of the destruction of Baltimore would be received in England with the greatest éclat—the tower gun would be fired and a general illumination would take place throughout the United Kingdom. Every window would be decorated with Warren's name, and he and Cockburn hailed as the most accomplished burglars and marauders of the age—and yet how confident are we of our safety! We meet, we converse, we complain of this man and of that man, of one public body and of another; we censure the conduct of this official character, and condemn that of another, but of what consequence is all this, and to what does it all amount? If the General Government is insensible of our danger—if the Governor of Maryland has neglected his duty, if the city is exposed, will our complaints, and our arguments and our repinings avail anything? Shall the city of Baltimore, destined to be the first in commercial importance on the continent calmly await the attack of the enemy and trust to the confusion with which must ensue, for the preservation of our property, and every thing which is dear to us in life? Shall a city of 40 or 50,000 inhabitants patiently acquiesce in the relinquishment of the little commerce which is left to it and even permit their usual market supplies to be cut off by a few British frigates, without an effort to keep the waters open? Are we bereft of our senses? And are we resolved to act only on the defensive? Are there no expedients to be tried?...The writer of this article is of the opinion that much can be done in the way of annoyance. The ingenuity of our citizens should be taxed as well as their purses.*[139]

The writer of the letter goes on to suggest that a general meeting of the citizens be held to brainstorm ideas and a committee appointed to see that donations are collected to support the efforts and to put their ideas in front of the government.

This letter highlights the real concerns of the nation's citizens during the War of 1812. Not only was this writer fearful of an attack on Baltimore, but he was also angry about the situation in which his government had placed him. He mentioned the financial hit the city's commercial market had taken because of the British presence in the Bay and called out the federal and state governments for neglecting their duty to provide adequate defense of their citizens' personal property. He also understood what a triumph the sacking of Baltimore would be for the British. It is doubtful even President Madison understood this point, judging from his laissez-faire handling of the war in the Bay.

Another article published on May 5 spoke on the same theme:

> *To the Citizens of Baltimore. We have been told that Admiral Cockburn was at Havre de Grace in person and has declared that he will either burn Baltimore, or die in the attempt. We have it from authority, on which we think we can rely, that he has absolutely declared his determination to destroy the city of Baltimore. And what is the common explanation of our citizens in reply to his observations? "Well let him come!!" Good Heavens! Is it possible that people, who have senses about them, who have lives at stake and property to lose, can be so phlegmatic at such a time? Who would not suppose that such indifference proceeded from a conviction that every arm was nerved, every body in armour, every spear was pointed, and every shield made impregnable? Who would not suppose that we were in a complete state of preparation, not only resolved to meet them at water's edge, but able to contest every inch of ground with effect? But is this the case? This is no time to parley—It is our duty to bring the subject home "to men's business and to their bosoms." Are all our citizens armed? Are preparations made for an alarm, in the event of a landing of the enemy in the night, without their being discovered at the fort? Is your watch in the city doubled and trebled? Is every vulnerable point guarded and protected against surprise? Has a meeting of the citizens been called and a committee been...*[140]

Much like the tragedies of the twenty-first century, the 1813 attack also inspired an outpouring of philanthropic support. Again, from the May 4 *Baltimore Patriot*:

> *It has been suggested that a subscription ought immediately to be made in this city, for the relief of the unhappy sufferers at Havre de Grace. Baltimore has never yet been remiss in her duty. Claims on the sympathy and on the patriotism of her citizens has never been disregarded. The manner in which*

the evil has come upon Havre de Grace, and the cause in which she has suffered, both conspire to awaken the most lively feelings of philanthropy.[141]

Although no record remains as to the results of such a collection, it is a nice sentiment that the city wanted to help out its neighbors to the north.

The *Niles' Weekly Register* captured everyone's anger at the attack in its May 8 issue:

Wanton outrage! Only a single house was left uninjured, and by far the greater parts are heaps of ruins. The history of civilized war, we are happy to say for the honour of human nature, presents few parallels for this barbarous outrage, so eminently characteristic of the British nation, immortal in the history of our revolution for exploits of the kind. There was no legitimate war *object to obtain by demolishing the* defenceless *village of Havre de Grace, and the attack was savage, directed only by that kind of feeling that impels an Indian in his wars. No resistance was made or offered; the village was surprised, the houses conflagrated by a coup de main, and old age and infancy involved in the general wreck. Something had been designed for the defence of the place, but the fatality that has attended the military movements of Maryland neglected to perform it. If such is the character of this contest, and Admirals Cockburn and Brigadier Tecumseh shall continue thus to violate all the known usages of honourable war, it is time indeed for the people to open their eyes to their true condition, and shut their ears to the Syren songs of British "religion and magnanimity." The ruins of Havre de Grace shall stand as a monument of British cruelty, in which, as in a glass, we may see the true spirit of the Government. The villain deed has roused the honest indignation of every man; no one pretends to justify or excuse it. It has knit the people into a common bond for vengeance on the incendiaries; it has destroyed party, and by a community of interests effected what patriotism demanded in vain.*[142]

However, not all British troops felt pride at the destruction of the towns along the Chesapeake. Said Lieutenant Colonel Charles Napier of the 102nd Regiment:

Strong is my dislike to what is perhaps a necessary part of our job, viz. plundering and ruining the peasantry. We drive all their cattle and of course ruin them; my hands are clean, but it is hateful to see the poor Yankees robbed, and to be the robber. If we should take fairly it would not be so bad, but the rich escape; for the loss of a few cows and oxen is nothing to a rich man, while you ruin a poor peasant if you take his only cow.[143]

In the repeated telling of the Havre de Grace story and the outrage it inspired, the numbers of buildings that were actually destroyed got distorted. Right after the attack, many reports (including the *Niles' Weekly Register*, reprinted earlier) said every building in Havre de Grace except for Mr. Pringle's home was burned to the ground. The exaggeration was likely from the shock of the attack as well as a propaganda technique employed by newspaper publishers to sensationalize the news and vilify the British.

Jared Sparks, the tutor who was living with Mr. Pringle in 1813, wrote his account of the attack four years later in 1817, in part to set right some of the rumors surrounding the event. One thing he specifically addressed was the extent of destruction: "It has been said in a very respectable history of the times, that one house only escaped the flames; but this is a mistake. Havre de Grace consisted of about sixty houses, and of these not more than forty were burnt. Many others were plundered and much injured, and scarcely one remained which was not perforated with balls or defaced by the explosion of shells."[144] So the British were thorough with their plundering more so than their burning, although that was not of any relief to the townspeople of Havre de Grace.

Meanwhile, several of their friends and family were still being held prisoner by the British on the *Maidstone*. Mr. Levy, a prisoner himself, and his sense of humor were an aid in their release. One story has it that Levy saw one of the British sailors wrapped up in a garment belonging to Havre de Grace's Mrs. Miers. Levy asked the sergeant for a pint, explaining that the former owner of the wrap had served him many a pint. The sergeant laughed heartily and gave Levy some grog.[145]

Back onshore, several neighbors banded together to try to free the prisoners, including Mr. Jarret, Mr. Dutton, Miss Oliver and Miss Matilda O'Neill, John O'Neill's fifteen-year-old daughter. They rowed out to the *Maidstone* in boats, with a flag of truce in hand, and once there, Matilda begged for her father's release. Legend has it that Admiral Cockburn was so impressed by Matilda's bravery in her father's interest that he gave her a tortoise-shell snuffbox and released all the prisoners. This story has never been definitively proven, although the snuffbox does exist in the collection of the Maryland Historical Society.

After releasing the prisoners, Cockburn was still docked at Specutia Island planning his next move. As the Sassafras River was the only area of the

The tortoise-shell snuffbox Matilda O'Neill received from Admiral Cockburn. *MDHS.*

Upper Bay he hadn't yet explored, and he knew that Fredericktown and Georgetown were both "places of some trade and importance," he decided they would be his next targets.[146] The townspeople in both places also knew they would be in his sights.

On the afternoon of May 5, Cockburn sailed his fleet up the Sassafras intending to destroy both towns. After the fact, he claimed he did not have designs on attacking either town unless he encountered opposition, but his ship's log specifically records his plans to destroy them.[147]

Like it did in its attack on Havre de Grace, the fleet loaded into boats and paddled up the Sassafras right after midnight on May 6. However, as the sun began to peek over the horizon, it became clear that the British were once again lost. They kidnapped a local man they encountered on the water, John Stavely, to serve as their river guide.

Not long afterward, they encountered two black boys, with whom Cockburn entrusted his message to the town: don't resist the British forces, and they will not harm you. He sent the boys ahead to deliver his message, reasoning the boys were known by the townspeople and would be believed.

Meanwhile, a call went out from Fredericktown for the Cecil County militia to muster, but only about eighty men arrived, and many with no muskets but only their fowling weapons. The men were able to assemble a small battery, although they only had one six-pounder mounted there and only two rounds of ammunition for it.

As the sun rose fuller in the sky, those manning the battery saw the fleet approaching. "The large barges had formed a line four abreast and several hundred yards long, but in close and compact order. In each were the splendidly attired Royal Marines sitting ramrod erect, with their scarlet jackets afire in the new morning sun."[148]

The two black boys landed at Fredericktown first, delivering their message to those in the battery, to no effect—most likely as Cockburn had hoped. The battery opened fire as soon as the British were within range. They mustered such force that Cockburn thought he was facing as many as four hundred men.[149] However, they were still no match for the British firepower. When they unleashed their guns and rockets, half the militia turned tail and ran. The rest stuck it out for an hour and only suffered one injury.

One eyewitness commented about the Congreve rockets—the same used at Havre de Grace: "I think I saw and heard four rockets flying at once, and they were, to be sure, to ear and eye most terrific, but they all fell harmless, and are now objects of but little terror to many of our militiamen."[150] However, when the Royal Navy landed with bayonets drawn, the militia's bravery deserted them, and they fled for the woods.

Cockburn then proceeded to set the town ablaze "excepting the houses of those who had continued peaceably in them and had taken no part in the attack made on us," as Cockburn explained to Warren.[151] Four vessels were destroyed, as well as stores of sugar, lumber, leather and other goods.

One victim at Fredericktown was John Allen, who testified:

> *The inside works of the clock…they took on board the barge…Then my meat house, small grainry boat and fish house, containing fifty barrels of salt-fish; all my bacon and one year's provisions…My family Bible and the life of Washington* [a book] *were taken away. Then the store was robbed of about $1200 in groceries; the heads of the liquor casks stove in, and mixed with molasses.*[152]

The buildings were then set ablaze. The plunder and burning continued on from one neighbor to the next, as it had in Havre de Grace.

Next on Cockburn's list was Georgetown, a larger town than Fredericktown but much less well defended. It was taken without a shot being fired, and the townspeople again fled into the distance as the British set to work plundering and burning each building. At least twenty-four businesses, shops, homes and storehouses were lost.

An 1813 sketch by British Lieutenant Henry Crease of the May 6 attack on Fredericktown (B) and Georgetown (C). *Library of Congress.*

It was during this attack that Miss Kitty Knight took her stand against Cockburn and became a local legend for it. She reportedly confronted the admiral after twice putting out fires at her home and told him that by burning her house, he would be endangering the elderly neighbor in the home next to hers. She won her argument, and both houses still stand today.

After spending the day terrorizing these two waterfront towns, Cockburn and his troops retired back to Specutia Island for the night. Feeling he had visited every town along the water in the Upper Bay, Cockburn decided it was time to head south to reunite with Warren's ships.

Newspapers around the nation lampooned Cockburn for his ruthless attacks, and people everywhere were calling for his head. One gentleman went so far as to offer a reward of $1,000 for the "head of the notorious incendiary and infamous scoundrel" or "$500 for each ear."[153]

While some people got mad and made outlandish bounty requests, Privateer Joshua Barney developed a plan. Writing to Secretary of the Navy William Jones, he calculated how many troops and seamen the British could unleash on the area and specifically stated his belief that the enemy's ultimate goal was to capture both Washington and Baltimore.[154] He proposed a flotilla using the same type of low boats the British had used to attack Havre de Grace that could maneuver in shallow water.

Barney's plan was approved by the naval secretary, but while the flotilla boats were under construction into 1814, the British attacks continued down the coast. The British tried sailing into Fort Washington during the summer of 1813 but ran into shallow waters. Unbelievably, President Madison and Secretary of War John Armstrong did not reinforce the capital area with troops at this point, still laboring under the delusion that the British were not interested in Washington because it was a backwater town.[155] As we now know, that was a decision that would come back to punish them in 1814.

The Burning of Washington

I n April 1814, British Admiral Warren was replaced by Sir Alexander Forrester Inglis Cochrane, with Cockburn still second in command of the British naval forces in the Chesapeake. The first few months of summer developed the same as the summer before, with the British plundering and burning towns along the edge of the Bay.

But one thing was different in the summer of 1814—American Captain Joshua Barney's flotilla was finally ready for action. At the end of May 1814, it headed south from Baltimore toward the British base on Tangier Island. Barney and Secretary William Jones had high hopes for the flotilla, with Jones telling Barney, "Your force is our principal shield," and Barney replying, "I am anxious to be at [the British]."[156]

Unfortunately, not too long after setting off, Barney's flotilla tangled with the British and found itself blockaded in St. Leonard's Creek, an offshoot of the Patuxent River. The First Battle of St. Leonard's Creek (June 8–10, 1814) involved the same Congreve rockets used in Havre de Grace. Once again, one landed on top of a man and killed him, as well as blew one of the flotilla boats to pieces. The Americans also managed to do some damage to the British fleet, but at the end of the battle, they were still blocked in the Patuxent with no way to escape.

In an effort to lure Barney out of the creek, the British set about plundering and burning the towns and plantations that lay along the Patuxent. It was readily clear that the attacks on Havre de Grace and its neighbors in the Upper Bay had served as practice for the violence now

Joshua Barney. *Library of Congress.*

being unleashed farther south. However, Barney didn't take the bait and continued to wait.

To assist in the Second Battle of Leonard's Creek (June 26, 1814), the American army arrived to reinforce the land positions around Barney. The battle ended with the flotilla escaping St. Leonard's Creek and rowing furiously up the Patuxent. Having lost Barney for the time being, the British went back to what they did best—plundering and burning. They attacked St. Leonard Town and at least five more towns.

After his series of successes attacking towns over the past twelve months, Cockburn was itching to hit America in the heart and capture its capital. However, his equivalent officer in command of the British army, Major General Robert Ross, wasn't as game—his land troops had arrived straight from the Peninsula Wars against Napoleon's forces "with no supporting artillery or cavalry and [were] ill-equipped for battle."[157] However, Cockburn was insistent and relied on his charm and persuasive nature to eventually convince the less-confident Ross to at least take a step in the direction of Washington.

The plan they hatched was to enter the Patuxent River and land the army at Benedict as a springboard for possible future operations into Washington. Ross wasn't ready to agree to an attack on the capital city, but he did see the importance of forcing Barney's flotilla out of the Patuxent.[158]

While Ross and Cockburn were finalizing their plans, American Secretary of State James Monroe was becoming nervous about the proximity of the British to the U.S. capital. Unlike President Madison and Secretary Armstrong, who did not believe the British would come for Washington and were not repositioning troops to defend the city, Monroe did believe the British were wily and brazen enough to try taking the capital. Launching his own scouting mission, his hunch was confirmed when, on August 20, he saw the British unload over four thousand men onto the Patuxent's shores.

Barney was advised that British troops were closing in on his flotilla, which was now blocked in the northern tip of the Patuxent River. He was given orders to blow up his fleet if the British closed in on him. Knowing destruction would be the ultimate fate of his beloved flotilla, he abandoned his ships and marched his troops west to join the American land forces, leaving behind a few men to scuttle the fleet.

It is of some comfort to all Americans to imagine the joy Cockburn must have felt when he discovered Barney's flotilla, bobbing in the water near Pig Point, and his utter dismay when the entire works blew up in front of him. First thinking he had captured the flotilla—men, boats and all—Cockburn soon "saw clearly that [the ships] were all abandoned and on fire with trains to the magaz[ines], and out of the seventeen vessels which composed this formidable and so much vaunted flotilla, sixteen were in quick succession blown to atoms."[159]

Despite their failure in capturing the flotilla, Cockburn's chase helped to conceal the British's real intent for their presence on the river: access to good roads to Washington.[160]

At this point, Cockburn convinced Ross that they were within striking distance of Washington and that they should advance and attack. He sent his aide-de-camp to their superior officer, Admiral Cochrane, with a message indicating his intentions, only to receive a response ordering him and Ross not to attack. But Cockburn was not to be deterred. He knew he was risking his career by disobeying orders, but he felt strongly that Washington was ripe for the taking.[161]

When morning dawned, the troops set off through oppressive heat that quickly drained the British in their woolen uniforms. Ross chose the northeastern route to Washington through Bladensburg, "partly to deceive the Americans but mainly to be able to cross the eastern branch of the Potomac [into Washington] without relying on the bridges."[162]

The British troops were met at Bladensburg on August 24 by ten thousand American men and artillery. Although the Americans looked formidable, Ross observed their lines from a distance and realized they were too far apart to support one another. He ordered an attack.

The first 1,400 British forces to charge suffered high casualties as the Americans unleashed their cannon on them. But as reinforcements moved in and British Congreve rockets screamed in the air, it was soon clear Ross's gamble had paid off. The untrained American militiamen soon broke rank and took off for the hills, earning the battle the moniker the "Bladensburg Races."

Commodore Joshua Barney fought on land during this battle and was injured in the leg. In an uncharacteristic show of sympathy, Rear Admiral Cockburn "consoled and reassured him while an English surgeon bound his wounds. Barney was promptly freed on parole, as were some of his officers, to see him to a place of safety. So deep an impression did this gesture make on the Commodore's mind that he resolved, on recovery, to return his thanks to Cockburn in person under a flag of truce."[163] Giving us a peek at his motive toward kindness, Cockburn was heard to say, "They gave us the only fighting we have had."[164]

At the end of the battle, the British had suffered more casualties than the Americans, but they still had their victory—there was nothing standing in the way between them and Washington.

In 1814, Washington had only been the government seat for fourteen years and still very much fit its nickname, "the Wilderness City." Most lawmakers lived in Georgetown, a more developed area in the northwest section of Washington along the Potomac. "A census a few years after the British attack showed Washington had a population of 13,247, comprising 9,607 white, 1,696 free blacks and 1,944 slaves."[165]

The Burning of Washington

British soldiers are shown in the foreground, with British ships in the background, as Washington (on the hill) is bombarded. *Library of Congress.*

Washington was shrouded in darkness when Ross and Cockburn arrived to find it deserted later the same day. They carried a flag of truce, hoping to spare the city—or possibly gain a handsome ransom. However, there was no one left to negotiate with—the president, statesmen, soldiers and residents had all escaped to the hills around the city.

A few people had stayed, and they chose to fire upon the British. "At this point Cockburn took charge, for the present situation bore a striking similarity to many he had experienced in his Chesapeake landings," explained Cockburn's biographer, James Pack. "Then he had respected private property and only when arms had been found or there had been resistance had he lit the torch."[166]

Pack's telling of the burning of Washington paints Cockburn in a sympathetic light, much in contrast to the view the Americans had of him, thanks to his reign of terror in the Chesapeake. Pack justifies Cockburn's decision to burn Washington in this way:

> *He was fully aware of the feeling in the higher ranks of the British service that, in this wholly unnecessary war declared by President Madison, the Americans had burned and plundered Canadian settlements and townships inhumanely. Retaliation was ever an unfortunate consequence of war but the decision was taken at this moment not to spare Washington's public buildings.*[167]

The Capitol building and the houses adjoining it were set on fire with the assistance of Congreve rockets, just as in Havre de Grace. Margaret Bayard

95

Capture and burning of Washington by the British. *Library of Congress.*

Smith, the wife of the Bank of Washington president, gave the following eyewitness account of the burning of the Capitol building: "50 men, sailors, and marines were marched by an officer, silently thro' the avenue...when arrived at the building. Each man was stationed at a window, with his pole and machine of wild-fire...the windows were broken and this wild fire was thrown in, so that an instantaneous conflagration took place and the whole building was wrapt [*sic*] in flames and smoke."[168]

Next up in flames were the archives and a library that was to become the Library of Congress. The British then set off for the White House. President and Mrs. Madison had already fled the White House but had left dinner piping hot on the dining room table. The British troops "could scarcely believe their luck: a supply of excellent Madeira and other wines considerably packed in their ice coolers, and food in plenty for the inner man awaited them. There was even fine china—and crystal goblets to help add to the sense of occasion as they slaked their thirst and toasted the Prince Regent."[169] After taking a few souvenirs from the executive mansion, the British set fire to it as well.

After Cockburn and Ross spent a few hours in Washington on the morning of August 25, surveying the damage they had done and setting

The Burning of Washington

U.S. Capitol after burning by the British. Drawing by George Munger, 1814. *Library of Congress.*

a few missed buildings alight, they decided it was time to withdraw their troops. Word had it that the Americans were amassing an army in Georgetown, and Ross's troops were too exhausted from the previous days' activities at Bladensburg to fight another battle.

As with Havre de Grace, word spread of the attack on Washington like wildfire, this time worldwide. Scathing criticisms were rampant around the nation—interestingly, many of them critical of the American governmental leaders who allowed such an attack to happen in the first place.

A message scrawled on the walls of the Capitol read, "George Washington founded this city after a seven year's war with England. James Madison lost it after a two years' war."[170] Another read, "Armstrong sold the city…The Capital of the Union lost by cowardice."[171]

Philadelphia's *United States Gazette* demanded the country's leaders be "constitutionally impeached and driven with scorn and execration from the seats which they have dishonored and polluted."[172]

Madison, who was reportedly brokenhearted at the turn of events, returned to the ruined city and issued a proclamation that the capital was back in the hands of the United States government. Madison's message also helped rally the citizens around the country in support of their nation, the United States. He keenly focused the blame away from his administration and onto the British.

What he and Armstrong had failed to grasp was that, despite its backwater appearance, Washington was still the capital of the United States. It was a significant triumph for the British to burn it and a great setback for the Americans in real estate, money and morale.

Meanwhile, Cochrane welcomed Ross and Cockburn back with high praise, apparently deciding to ignore their blatant insubordination. Upon his great success at capturing Washington, Cockburn suggested they next set their sights on Baltimore. Both Ross and Cochrane agreed.

THE DEFENSE OF BALTIMORE

T he townspeople of Baltimore knew that an attack on their city was likely after the past year of action by the British up and down the Chesapeake Bay. They knew that Baltimore's successful port, and its nest of privateers who had made trouble for the British from the start, would be an enticing target for Cockburn. Plus, they were the third-largest city in the nation, after New York and Philadelphia. The total ruin of Washington was a wake-up call, and Baltimoreans set to work on a defense for the city.

They found their leader in Samuel Smith, a local decorated Revolutionary War hero. Ironically, it was Smith and his brother who had given John Rodgers his first job as a captain of their merchant ship *Jane* all those years ago. Now they would become colleagues in this integral battle.

> *Newly-minted Major General Smith used all his energy, leadership, and prestige to get the entire community working together in a united cause. Nothing escaped his attention: raising funds; laying rings of defense on land and water; recruiting, equipping, and supplying thousands of militiamen from all over the region; seeking scarce federal help, as available; and most important of all, keeping Baltimore's spirit in fighting trim.* [173]

Despite the obvious need for city defense after the disaster in Washington, federal funds still didn't exist. The defense of Baltimore was financed by private contributions totaling about $15,000, as well as with state aid.[174] After some encouragement from Smith, the local banks provided an additional $663,000.[175]

Smith anticipated the British would attack by both land and water. He ordered the townspeople to dig earthworks as fortifications at North Point, which they did in shifts by neighborhood. When John Rodgers arrived in town after helping to restore order to Washington, he put his marines to work digging beside the citizens. He also ordered his men still on the water to sink hulls to block the waterways in the harbor.

Rodgers combined his three hundred seamen with five hundred flotilla men who were already in Baltimore to form a brigade, which he sat out in the harbor as conspicuously as possible.[176] The presence of Rodgers and the marines calmed the fears of the Baltimoreans and even inspired them with a patriotic spirit.[177]

Members of the Harford County militia were called into service for the defense of Baltimore on August 27 and marched to Hampstead Hill (now Patterson Park). This group included men from Havre de Grace who would finally have the opportunity to avenge the attack on their town from over a year earlier.[178]

The Harford regiments of militia were the Fortieth and the Forty-second, and most men camped along with thousands of other militiamen on Hampstead Hill above the city. Upon arriving in camp, each man received a kettle, mess pan, spade, axe and straw for bedding.[179] Details of the daily rations for the infantry are found in Thomas A. Hays's papers: "Captain entitled to three rations; Lieutenant to two, ensign to two. A ration is 1¼ pounds of beef or ¾ of pork; 18 ounces of loaf bread (or flour) or ¾ pound of navy bread; one gill of whiskey; and at the rate of 4 pounds soap, 4 quarts vinegar, 2 quarts salt and ½ pound of candles to every 100 men."[180]

Baltimore continued its preparations and waited nervously through the end of August and the first ten days of September. The city was crowded with fifteen thousand militiamen waiting for the British to make their move.

Then, on the morning of Sunday, September 11, the British fleet was spotted near North Point. The cannon on the green fired their warning, causing an immediate dismissal from church services. Militiamen ran for their positions. Women and children escaped out of town. Baltimore was in bedlam.[181]

Commodore John Rodgers and his marines were stationed on Hampstead Hill when the warning alarm sounded. An entry from a member of the Sixteenth Regiment, Matthias E. Bartgis, explains the commodore's actions there:

About 2 o'clock P.M., our company, with some others, composing the first Battalion of the first Regiment, were selected to be placed as flankers,

The Defense of Baltimore

Assembly of Troops before the Battle of Baltimore. Oil of canvas by Thomas Ruckle Sr., circa 1814. *MDHS.*

with two Battalions of Riflemen on our right, all under the command of Commodore Rodgers, we were placed in battle order, in the rear of the battery on the right of the entrenchments and so remained for that day and night. The Battery was called Rodgers' Battery and manned with sailors and marines, commanded by Naval Officers.[182]

As he had done since his arrival in Baltimore, Rodgers instilled bravery and order in the troops under his command. The humor of his situation—a seaman leading a land battle—did not escape him. He wrote to his wife, Minerva, "If you were to see what a figure I cut with spurs on…on horseback, you'd split your sides laughing."[183]

Upon hearing the news of the British landing, General Smith ordered Baltimore's Third Brigade under Brigadier General John Stricker to North Point, and the troops marched down the streets of the city "with flags flying, bands playing, and crowds cheering."[184] They arrived at North Point around 8:00 p.m. that evening.

At 3:00 a.m. on September 12, about 4,700 British began to land at the tip of Patapsco Neck at North Point. Stricker learned that Cockburn, Ross and their men were having a leisurely breakfast at the home of one of the locals and, assuming their actions were motivated by arrogance, responded by sending out 150 of his advance troops in the direction of the home.

Meanwhile, Cockburn and Ross had finished their meal and were headed for Baltimore with their advance troops, when Americans concealed in the woods opened fire and struck General Ross. Henry McComas and Daniel Wells, both still teenagers, were credited with firing the shots that mortally wounded Ross. Unfortunately, they were both almost immediately gunned down by the redcoats and died. The loss of Ross was a painful one for the British and possibly changed the course of the battle. He was replaced with Colonel Arthur Brooke, who was nowhere near as confident of a leader as Ross had been.

The British suffered heavy casualties at North Point although they gained a little ground. The next day, they resumed marching and encountered a shocking sight—Hampstead Hill in the distance, covered with over ten thousand American militiamen. Brooke knew he was outmatched.

Around this time, he also received word from Cochrane that the naval assault on Fort McHenry was not going well and that Brooke would have to take the city without naval support. Fearing heavy casualties with little chance for success, especially during the raging storm nature was inflicting on the area, Brooke decided to retreat.

The thousands of militiamen camped at Hampstead Hill, including those from Havre de Grace, never saw any fighting. However, they were still instrumental in the city's win over the British by contributing to the large number of forces that frightened the enemy away.

Next, it was Major Armistead's turn to hold Fort McHenry. He had about one thousand troops with him in the small fort. The British ships under the command of Admiral Cochrane opened fire on the fort at 6:00 a.m. on September 13 and continued all day and night. Congreve rockets were used, as well as heavy artillery and ammunition that was able to fly longer distances in hopes of reaching the fort.

The bombing put on a spectacular light and sound show that some townspeople watched from their rooftops. Others ran from the town with nothing more than their children and the clothes on their backs.

After firing on the fort for eighteen hours, Cochrane ordered an advance but was driven back by heavy American fire. He then ordered some of his ships to flank the fort, but they were met by about fifty of Joshua Barney's flotilla men under the command of Harford County resident Sailing Master John Adams Webster. The flanking ships were quickly forced back to rejoin the main fleet.

With Brooke's land troops having already retreated to their ships off North Point, Cochrane called off the bombardment at 7:00 a.m. on September 14. As the sounds of bombing ceased, all eyes on Hampstead Hill turned toward the fort to see if the American flag still flew. "When the morning mists had sufficiently dispersed, we were filled with exultation at beholding

Above: *A view of the bombardment of Fort McHenry, near Baltimore, by the British fleet, taken from the observatory under the command of Admirals Cochrane & Cockburn, on the morning of the 13th of September 1814.* Engraving by John Bower. *Library of Congress.*

Right: Francis Scott Key. *MDHS.*

the stars and stripes still floating in the breeze," said Private John Leadley Dagg, summarizing the pride felt by all the men on the hill that morning.[185]

Also seeing the flag floating above the fort that morning was American Francis Scott Key, who was out on one of the British ships, awaiting his release after the battle ended. A lawyer, Key had sailed out to the British fleet to negotiate the release of an American prisoner, and while he was successful, he and the prisoner had not been not allowed to leave the ship during the battle. The British feared they would share battle secrets with the Americans if released from the ship.

And so it was from a British ship in the harbor that Francis Scott Key witnessed the American flag flying over Fort McHenry that historic morning and penned the poem "The Defence of Fort M'Henry." His words would go on to become the United States' national anthem. It is true that Key wrote the lines to fit with the tune "To Anacreon in Heaven," an eighteenth-century English drinking song that was also popular in America.

Key's original poem had four verses, but only the first is widely known:

O say can you see by the dawn's early light,
What so proudly we hailed at the twilight's last gleaming,
Whose broad stripes and bright stars through the perilous fight,
O'er the ramparts we watched, were so gallantly streaming?
And the rockets' red glare, the bombs bursting in air,
Gave proof through the night that our flag was still there;
O say does that star-spangled banner yet wave,
O'er the land of the free and the home of the brave? [186]

Although most people don't realize it, the British tool of terror, the Congreve rocket, is specifically mentioned in the poem as "the rockets' red glare." The song became known as "The Star-Spangled Banner" and was played in the United States after the War of 1812, during the Civil War and into the nineteenth century, when America suddenly realized it didn't have a national anthem. John Philip Sousa proposed "The Star-Spangled Banner," and it was voted into law in 1931, over one hundred years after it was first written.

Another American icon came out of the defense of Baltimore—the Star-Spangled Banner itself. Major George Armistead commissioned the large garrison flag measuring thirty feet by forty-two feet, and a smaller storm flag at seventeen feet by twenty-five feet, to be sewn. Baltimore local Mary Pickersgill, an experienced flag maker, got the job.

The Defense of Baltimore

Mary Pickersgill Making the Star-Spangled Banner. By R. McGill Mackall, circa 1976. *MDHS.*

Mary, her thirteen-year-old daughter Caroline, her nieces (thirteen- and fifteen-year-olds Eliza and Margaret Young) and an indentured servant worked for seven weeks sewing the flag bunting. When it came time to piece together the enormous flag, they spread it out on the floor of a local brewery to sew the final rectangle.

The large garrison flag is the one that everyone in Baltimore saw the morning after the bombardment, but it was likely the smaller storm flag that actually flew during the battle. It is believed the men manning the fort replaced the storm flag with the large flag in the morning after winning the battle.

The Star-Spangled Banner is unique in comparison to the other flags the United States has used over the years. First, it has fifteen stars in the blue field representing the fifteen states that were in the nation during the War of 1812. Secondly, the stars are "spangled," which means they do not all face the same direction and are tilted at angles. Third, it is the only version of the American flag to have a red stripe under the blue field instead of a white stripe.

The Star-Spangled Banner. *Library of Congress.*

The Star-Spangled Banner is on display at the National Museum of American History in Washington, D.C., and was recently restored to help protect its threadbare material. The holes in the flag were created in the nineteenth century by people cutting out souvenir pieces.

As the people of Baltimore—and the nation—celebrated the win against the British forces, Commodore John Rodgers's heroic actions were not forgotten.

The Defense of Baltimore

The citizens of Baltimore presented a service of plates to him, each with the inscription: "Presented by the citizens of Baltimore to COM. JOHN RODGERS, in testimony of their high sense of the important aid afforded by him in the defence [*sic*] of Baltimore, on the 12th and 13th of September, 1814."[187]

A newspaper account about the plate presentation goes on to say:

> *Never was such a compliment more honestly, more faithfully, earned—never was one presented with a deeper interest and feeling than this occasion will give rise to. The unwearied volunteer-like services of Com. Rodgers in the defence* [sic] *of Baltimore, in Sept. 1814, were as a host in strength—teaching by example, spreading confidence every where, and infusing into each breast a portion of his own invincible spirit.*[188]

Despite their victory, Baltimoreans were worried the British would return, and they stayed in camp at Hampstead Hill until October. Several other battles took place around the country as 1814 drew to a close, as well as the Battle of New Orleans in early January 1815. Andrew Jackson led the Americans to a victory in this battle, securing for himself a place in the American history books as president in 1829.

The Signing of the Treaty of Ghent. Oil on canvas, Sir Amedee Forestier, circa 1914. *Smithsonian American Art Museum.*

However, the Treaty of Ghent that officially ended the War of 1812 had been signed on Christmas Eve 1814. Word of the peace didn't make it to either the Americans or the British in New Orleans before the fighting began, so the last battle of the war actually took place after the peace treaty had been signed.

The War of 1812 was instrumental in binding the citizens of the United States together around the cause of one nation. Prior to this war, they thought of themselves as residents of their towns and states and not as citizens of the United States. The War of 1812 changed that perception. The war also proved to Americans that they were able to stand up to the mighty British—not just once but twice—and come out victorious. Although neither the Americans nor British really won the war, it was a major boost for the morale of the people of the United States.

Rebuilding
Havre de Grace

E ven while the war raged on in Washington and Baltimore in 1814, the townspeople of Havre de Grace started to put their lives back together in the days following the attack in May 1813.

Historians are very lucky to have three firsthand accounts of the attack on Havre de Grace, along with a lot of other primary and secondary source material. We don't have to do too much guesswork on what went on—although the location and quantity of batteries still eludes us.

Unfortunately, we do not have the same wealth of information on how Havre de Grace rebuilt itself after the fire. Even though Jared Sparks wrote his account of the attack in 1817, four years after it occurred, he does not include any detail of the rebuilding efforts. It is understandable that the townspeople did not keep track of how they rebuilt; they were too busy rebuilding to keep records. Only a few traces left behind give us clues as to what happened in Havre de Grace.

One is a comment at the end of Daniel Mallory's story: "Some months after, while removing the rubbish for a new foundation for the tavern house, several parts of spoons were dug up, which were known to belong to us by the marks on the handles. These Mrs. Sears was kind enough to send to us; but they had become of very little value."[189]

Another is from the town council minutes, which were summarized in the early 1900s by William Preston. He states that the town council held a meeting in January 1813 (prior to the attack) to elect commissioners; however, the next note says that no meetings were held the rest of the year. In 1814, a survey was paid for with the remaining money in the treasury, with two men instructed to "hire chain carriers, procure stones, and to have the same set up at the four corners of each and every square as soon as the said corners are ascertained."[190] We also know a tax assessment was conducted in 1814. We can assume both of these activities were aimed at beginning to rebuild the town.

In May 1815, Thomas Courtney offered to furnish six hundred stones for the street corners at fifteen cents each, and his bid was accepted. He was then authorized to "haul, set up the stones, and dig the holes for the corner stones." Additionally, the town rented "Market Space and all the streets and alleys intersecting" to John Dunn for seven years.[191]

Short of a new discovery of a diary from this time in an archive or attic somewhere, we can only use common sense to piece together what happened. The other tool that would be useful in clarifying items such as where the batteries were located is archaeology. However, this science is expensive and, in this case, impractical for a town that has developed so much in the past two hundred years. We do have some architectural evidence in the three structures we know survived the fire: the Elizabeth Rodgers House, the Aveilhe-Goldsborough House and St. John's Church. These three buildings stand today, and their architectural details have been studied to place them in the early nineteenth century.

The Elizabeth Rodgers House at 226 North Washington Street is the oldest structure in Havre de Grace, dating from 1788. Its historical significance derives from its age and from the fact that it was owned by the Rodgers family, one of the most famous families in Havre de Grace. This home survived the flames of the British, even though it was supposedly extinguished three separate times. Much of the interior of the home has been changed, but the outside retains its nineteenth-century façade.[192]

The Aveilhe-Goldsborough House stands at 300 North Union Avenue and boasts a French style, having originally been built in 1801 by a Frenchman named John Baptiste Aveilhe. At the time of the British attack on Havre de Grace, it is believed that Mr. Goldsborough had just bought the house but did not yet live there. The Wilmer account states that Goldsborough lost all the furniture for his new house, as it was being stored at Alexander Rodgers's store. Also, the account states that a cannonball flew through the front wall of Goldsborough's new home, and the Aveilhe-Goldsborough House does indeed have evidence remaining of where a cannonball came through the wall. According to the minutes of the commissioners' meeting, Goldsborough was a prosperous merchant, the owner of several ships and

The Elizabeth Rodgers House as it appears today. *Author's photo*.

The Aveilhe-Goldsborough House as it appears today. *Author's photo.*

a store. In addition, he was responsible for the purchase of lumber and wood for the new town wharf, which was completed in 1831. The Aveilhe-Goldsborough House remained in the family from 1816 to 1855 and still stands today.[193]

St. John's Church as it appears today. *Author's photo.*

St. John's Church is located at 114 North Union Avenue. Even though the British destroyed the interior of the church during the attack, they did leave the walls standing. The town rebuilt the building, although it wasn't completed until 1831. During the construction, the church often functioned without a rector due to a lack of funds. Another fire in 1832 again reduced the church to just walls, and again it was rebuilt. Although some changes were made to the building through the centuries, the majority of the church today still appears as it did in 1813.[194]

Additionally, the Nicholas and Gabriel Sutor House at 121 South Washington Street is believed to be one of the only wood frame structures that survived the fire and stands today. Nicholas Sutor (or Suder) was a member of St. John's Church, and the tax assessments of 1798 and 1814 both include him as owning a one-story frame dwelling. The dwelling standing on his lot today is made almost entirely of wooden frame.

Based on the analysis of land deeds and architectural details, experts are able to make some educated guesses about other homes in town that may have survived the attack. Located at 140 St. John Street, the Joshua Green house is a likely survivor. It is a log structure, and logs were used as a building material in the nineteenth century, due to Havre de Grace's role as a reshipment port for timber from Pennsylvania. Land records show that Joshua Green received lots 161 and 152 from Samuel Jay in 1808. The 1814 tax assessment lists a two-story dwelling house of wood with a one-story addition by Joshua Green. It is possible this 1814 structure was rebuilt after he lost a structure in the fire, although we know a building stood on that lot when he bought it in 1808. Only archaeology could tell us for sure.[195]

The Old Ordinary at 100 St. John Street is another interesting building from a historical standpoint. This lot was owned by the McCaskeys in 1802 and was purchased by George Bartol in 1809. We know that Bartol was in town during the 1813 attack because he was mentioned in the Wilmer account. Wilmer, however, placed Bartol's dwelling farther north between Sears's and Mansfield's Taverns. We also know that Bartol owned a tavern in the 1830s. It is possible he operated the Old Ordinary building as a tavern in the 1810s and 1820s, although whether it was built before or after the fire would require additional research.[196]

Today, a town committee, in conjunction with the bicentennial of the 1813 attack, is researching some other homes to determine when they were built and if they survived the attack. These include the Thompson House (127 North Stokes Street), the Poplar House (308 St. John Street), the Barnes-Boyd House (301 St. John Street), the McCaskey Double House (366 and 368 Congress Avenue), the Joseph Carver House (117 South Washington Street), the Currier House (800 Market Street) and the Jacksteit House (814 South Market Street).[197]

The Old Ordinary Building as it appears today. *Author's photo.*

The Lafayette Hotel (501 St. John Street), while not the original building, definitely stands on the land, and possibly even the foundation, of Mrs. Sears's Tavern, which was burned down in the British attack. The land was deeded to the Havre de Grace Ferry Company in 1818.

The following seems to be an announcement about a purchase by the Havre de Grace Ferry Company in 1817, copied from the files of the Harford County Historical Society, although it is unattributed: "Pringle, Sappington, R.Y. Stokes, et al—purchased from William B. Stokes ten water lots on which stood the brick tavern lately burnt down with the stables now remain—thereon and the walls and materials together with the wharf and all the said William B. Stokes right of ferriage across the river Susquehanna. March 17, 1817."[198] We also know that Robert Smith was an investor in the Havre de Grace Ferry Company.

The current building on this land was built around 1835 by then-owner Abraham Jarrett Thomas as his residence. The Philadelphia, Wilmington and Baltimore Railway bought the land in 1856 and began to operate the building as the Lafayette Hotel. It currently serves as the American Legion building.[199]

The Lafayette Hotel was likely built on the foundation of Mrs. Sears's Tavern and today serves as the American Legion Building. *Author's photo.*

The history of John O'Neill's house is also interesting. The town hero's home stood on prime real estate fronting Washington Street (now 218 South Washington). He received this land from William B. Stokes in 1805, and his nail factory was across the street from his home. A description of the home in February 1814, less than a year after the burning of the town, lists the property owned by the "brave" John O'Neill as follows: "one lot in Havre de Grace containing one fifth of an acre with one dwelling house thereon of wood of one story, 22 feet by 18 feet, valued at $250.00." Although the house as it stands today has been changed quite a bit, the basement of the original house is about the same size as those measurements given in 1814. In O'Neill's will, he left the home to his son, and it remained in the O'Neill family for 158 years.[200]

Another interesting home is the Motz House. Although it is believed to have been built around 1838, an architectural examination found "hand-hewn, pegged timbers" that are believed to have been salvaged from the burning in 1813. This house stands at 715 North Stokes Street.[201] Other homes in the area believed to have been built around the same time include the Wollen Double House (522 and 524 North Adams Street), the Barnes-

The John O'Neill House as it appears today. *Author's photo.*

Hopper House (701 North Adams Street) and the McCabe House (718 North Stokes Street).[202]

The histories of these historic homes, all catalogued by the Maryland Historical Trust, give us small peeks into the bigger picture of how Havre de Grace rebuilt. First, we know from the anecdote about the spoons found at Mrs. Sears's Tavern that the townspeople came back and dug through the remains of their homes. Those who were homeless likely stayed with friends and neighbors who were more fortunate and hadn't lost their houses. Others may have relocated to Baltimore or other areas of Harford County to take jobs and make money. Slowly but surely, houses began to be rebuilt on the foundations where they once stood or on lots that hadn't been developed prior to the attack.

A significant piece of undeveloped land, Concord Point, was selected in 1827 for the location of a new lighthouse, needed to prevent ships from running aground in the river and Bay. John O'Neill was appointed by the federal government as the lighthouse keeper in recognition of his heroic acts

The Concord Point Lighthouse as it appears today. *Author's photo.*

during the attack on Havre de Grace. The lighthouse was built on Concord Point in 1827 by John Donohoo, a member of the Maryland militia who fought in the War of 1812 and a contractor who helped rebuild Havre de Grace in the years after the attack. A dwelling house for the lighthouse

The lighthouse keeper's house as it appears today. *Author's photo.*

keeper was built in 1826 about two hundred feet from the lighthouse. After John O'Neill died in 1838, members of his family continued to keep the light until it became automated in the 1920s.[203]

As the town came back to life, new infrastructure was needed. To that end, the town erected a new school in 1821 at the corner of St. Clair Street (now Pennington Avenue) and Union Avenue. The building was twenty-two feet by thirty feet. By 1830, enrollment at the school had reached 130 students.[204]

In 1840, a combined market house and school was built on Congress Avenue near Washington and Market Streets. The thirty-foot by seventy-five-foot building used its lower floor as a market and storage room, while the upstairs served as a council chamber and school. Seven grades of students were taught between this building and the one on Union Avenue.[205]

As discussed, we have a general idea of which houses survived the attack, but what happened to the personalities of the War of 1812? We know John O'Neill and his family rebuilt their home and received the new light keeper's house. In addition, O'Neill's tale spread throughout the country, and he was known as a hero for the rest of his days. He received a ceremonial sword from the people of Philadelphia, with an inscription

The presentation sword presented to John O'Neill. *MDHS.*

reading, "Presented to the gallant John O'Neill for his valor at Havre de Grace, by Philadelphia—1813." On the 100th anniversary of the attack, the town dedicated a cannon monument in his honor.

As for Commodore John Rodgers, in February 1815, he was appointed to head the newly established Board of Navy Commissioners. While in this post, he continued his tradition of innovating for the U.S. Navy, including the

This cannon monument stands near the lighthouse as a tribute to John O'Neill. It was dedicated on the 100th anniversary of the attack on Havre de Grace. *Author's photo.*

establishment of naval hospitals, the organization of the Depot of Charts and Instruments and the idea of a Naval Academy to provide on-the-job training and staff a professional navy. He died in 1837 of cholera but left a long line of family members who also served in the navy. His son Rear Admiral John Rodgers II (1812–1882), his grandson Vice-Admiral William Ledyard Rodgers (1860–1944) and his great-grandson Commodore John Rodgers (1881–1926) all served.

Another one of Commodore Rodgers and Minerva's sons, Robert Smith Rodgers, went into the army, but he married into another important naval family, the Perrys. Robert's wife, Sarah, was the daughter of Commodore Matthew C. Perry, the man who "opened Japan to the Western world."[206] Perry had served under Commodore Rodgers during the Barbary Wars, and the pair were likely the reason their two children met. Robert and Sarah were the grandparents of Calbraith Perry Rodgers (1879–1912), the man who made the first transcontinental airplane flight in 1911. Calbraith and his cousin John Rodgers (the commodore's great-grandson) single-handedly built a plane and flew it from Annapolis to Sion Hill, "which caused no little stir in Havre de Grace."[207] Sadly, both men ended up dying in plane crashes.

One of the commodore's brothers, George Washington Rodgers, also served in the navy and sired a line of navy men as well. Descendants of the Rodgers family continued to live at Sion Hill, and the home is still owned by the family today.

Unfortunately, Samuel Hughes did not have as glorious of an outcome to his 1813 experience. After the British burned Hughes's Principio Iron Foundry to the ground and destroyed all his cannon, he suffered great financial hardship. He rebuilt the ironworks by borrowing heavily from Robert Smith and Baltimore merchant Robert Gilmor. However, he was unable to pay his debts and had to sell his home, Mount Pleasant, to satisfy his creditors. Principio also passed to his creditors in 1817. It is safe to say the British attack ruined Samuel Hughes.

"Indeed, as one of only several cannon manufacturers to receive a government contract in the 1790s, Samuel Hughes' cannon factory was nationally important to the United States, and its destruction was a major coup for [Cockburn]," writes historian Christopher George. "In retrospect, the destruction of Principio had greater significance than the action at Havre de Grace, which was more important for cowing the people of the Chesapeake."[208] The Principio Iron Foundry lay in a state of ruin until 1836, when it was purchased and rebuilt by Joseph Whitaker II, a former ironmaster at the foundry, and his brother George.[209]

Poor Mark Pringle also didn't have very good luck after the attack. Pringle was a rich man because he was not afraid to take large business risks. He owned a significant amount of land and served as the director of the Susquehanna Canal Company. His home, Bloomsbury, survived the burning of Havre de Grace, and he continued to live there and conduct his business dealings. However, his "large business risks" must not have been entirely on the up-and-up, because in 1819, he was lynched by Baltimore businessmen in a "sinister mob action."[210]

Transportation helped Havre de Grace and the Upper Bay recover from the British attacks, just as it had helped the area grow in prominence during the colonial days. Only two months after the attacks in 1813, the first steamboat churned its way up the Chesapeake on its way to Frenchtown. One can visualize the large boat on the water: "Two half-round wooden boxes, one on either side of the craft, concealed from view a pair of giant sidewheel paddles that the engines turned to propel the craft, even against the wind and tide. On the sides of the paddle boxes

The Susquehanna Lock House, the home of the lockmaster for the canal, as it appears today. *Author's photo.*

could be seen in elegant, brightly painted letters the words Union Line and Chesapeake."[211]

The steamboat ushered in a new era of transportation and renewed commerce for the small towns that lined the waterways. Because the boats weren't slaves to the winds and tides, as the ferries had been, they began regular runs to Frenchtown three times a week, where passengers could then board a stagecoach to New Castle and then another steamboat to Philadelphia. This traffic made Frenchtown a place of importance for shipping and stagecoach operations. Farmers sold grain, horses and feed to the stagecoach operators, and hotels would buy food and supplies for their guests.[212]

Meanwhile, by the late 1830s, two other types of transportation were having an economic impact on Havre de Grace, bringing money and new residents to the area. Both the railroad and the canal had come to town.

The Susquehanna River was an important waterway for the transportation of goods out of rural Pennsylvania to the ports of Baltimore. However, it was rocky and shallow, which made navigation nearly impossible. The Susquehanna and Tidewater Canal was built from Wrightsville, Pennsylvania, to Havre de Grace in order for timber, coal, wheat and other products to travel to port.[213]

Twenty-nine locks were constructed along the length of the canal that served as elevators to step the boats up and down the river by controlling the amount of water in the locks. A towpath—a dirt road along the canal—allowed mules to pull the barges up and down the canal between locks. An item printed in the *Baltimore American* in May 1840 demonstrated the importance of the canal system: "Yesterday four canal boats arrived here in Baltimore from Havre de Grace. Their arrival constituted the coming of a new era in the commerce of our city. Return cargoes may now be sent, consisting of groceries, dry goods, sugar, coffee, salt fish, and plaster. Our merchants may now extend their operations with safety, and they may purchase produce to any extent."[214]

Great expansion was occurring in the city as the canal was getting underway, and businessmen began speculating in land, much as they had done at the turn of the nineteenth century. A speech made aboard the steamboat *Carroll* in 1840 proclaimed Havre de Grace was "soon to become the depot of the Western World"—and this was said less than thirty years after having been burned by the British.[215]

The railroad also made its appearance in Havre de Grace around the same time as the canal. A line called the Baltimore and Port Deposit Railroad began in Baltimore in 1834 and had been completed as far as Havre de Grace by 1836. By 1838, the Philadelphia, Wilmington & Baltimore Railroad (PW&B) had been completed in the northern direction and absorbed the Baltimore and Port Deposit Railroad.

Interestingly, the Susquehanna River caused problems for the trains. It was too large for a bridge, so for nearly thirty years, the train cars had to be ferried across the river. The first bridge crossing the Susquehanna was erected with wood and put into use in 1866. From 1873 to 1878, it was gradually converted to steel and was used until 1939. The PW&B was absorbed into the Pennsylvania line, which began to use a new bridge in 1908.

Those familiar with Maryland history may be surprised to learn that the Baltimore & Ohio Railroad (B&O) was not the first line into Havre de Grace. In fact, the B&O did not begin building northward track until 1880 and did not reach Harford County until 1885. It built its own bridge across the Susquehanna in Havre de Grace, about a half mile north of the PW&B bridge, with its piers resting on Palmer's Island. This resulted in the renaming of the island to Garrett's Island in honor of B&O President John W. Garrett.

The building of the railroad bridge from Perryville to Havre de Grace. *HSHC.*

The B&O Railroad Station at the top of a hill on the right side of Ontario Street above Angel Hill Cemetery, circa 1900. *HSHC.*

The Sappington House as it appeared around the turn of the twentieth century. *HSHC.*

The building of the locks, canal and railroad bridges brought many laborers to town, who stayed and raised their families in Havre de Grace. As a result, schools, churches and shops flourished.

Several brick, Greek Revival mansions were built in town at this time, the Sappington House at 212 South Union being one of them. The design of these homes was meant to "reflect the material prosperity which was expected to arise from the canal, railroad, and the location of the town as a port of reshipment."[216] Other mansions included the Hall House at 227 South Union and the Hoke House at 213 South Union.[217]

Industry was also springing up in town. George, Joseph and John Price Whitaker, the men who had purchased Hughes's Principio Iron Foundry, built two iron furnaces at the foot of Bourbon Street around 1845 as an adjunct to their large furnaces at Principio.[218] They were built after the construction of the PW&B Railroad, allowing for better shipping access than their Principio location provided.

Other early industries in the area included oyster and crab harvesting, ice cutting and shipping and commercial fishing. Canning houses were built for packing corn and tomatoes, which provided employment for

The Sappington House today. *Author's photo.*

The Silverstein House around 1900. *HSHC.*

hundreds of people.[219] The area also became popular for duck hunting and the art of decoy carving, something Havre de Grace is well known for still today.

By the 1860s, the town had become an active terminal for the reshipment of lumber, coal and grain served by the canal, steamships and railroad. James Hopper was a wealthy businessman with a coal and wood business at the end of Otsego Street, near the canal. He built a large house for himself at 605 Ontario Street, a mixed Italianate and Greek Revival mansion.[220] Similar homes of the period were the Carver-Coburn House (453 Congress Avenue)[221] and the Silverstein House (414 Congress Avenue), which had a unique Italianate rectangular belvedere on its roof.[222]

The Seneca Cannery (201 St. John Street) was built in 1880 by Stephen J. Seneca as the headquarters for his fruit packing and can manufacturing business. The building was designed by John Donahoo, who had built the Concord Point Lighthouse nearly fifty years prior, and was located right along the water's edge to make for easy shipping. In turn, Stephen Seneca built a Victorian mansion in 1885 to show off his wealth. The home, at 200 North Union Avenue, features copper-covered turrets, bay windows, dormers and porches and faces Union Avenue, the most important street in the city.[223]

The Seneca Mansion as it appears today. *Author's photo.*

A second mansion built around the same time as the Seneca Mansion was the Vandiver Mansion at 301 South Union Avenue. This home is an example of Queen Anne architecture and was built by Murray Vandiver. He and his brother were coal trans-shippers, but he also served as the contractor for the Lapidum canal lock and the railroad cut that led down to the river. Additionally, he had a storied political career in the state of Maryland and also as the mayor of Havre de Grace.[224]

The third grand house built during this time was the Spencer-Silver Mansion at 200 South Union Avenue. This home is a high Victorian stone mansion, built in 1896 to reflect the wealth and position of owner John Spencer, who was in the fish packing business. These three homes are a

The Spencer-Silver Mansion as it appears today. *Author's photo.*

visually stunning reminder of the considerable wealth of Havre de Grace citizens at turn of the century.[225]

And so it was that, by the end of the nineteenth century, Havre de Grace had rebuilt and found success again, thanks to the same element that had made it great one hundred years prior: its location as a natural center for transportation and commerce.

By the end of the 1800s, the War of 1812 had largely been forgotten, due to another war that had taken place from 1861 to 1865: the Civil

War. Havre de Grace had managed to rebuild from Cockburn's terror and return to its destiny as a thriving town nestled at the junction of the Chesapeake Bay and the Susquehanna River. But the town will never completely forget the attack of the British; the lighthouse stands as a reminder of John O'Neill's heroism. Plus, the townspeople of today's Havre de Grace, through important celebrations like the 200th anniversary of the attack, will continue to keep the story alive for generations to come.

NOTES

FINDING HAVRE DE GRACE

1. Montgomery, "Captain John Smith."
2. Rountree, Clark and Mountford, *John Smith's Chesapeake Voyages*, 53.
3. Smith in *Captain John Smith*, ed. Kupperman, 160.
4. Wright, *Our Harford Heritage*, 159.
5. Alsop, *Province of Maryland*, 79.
6. Ibid., 67.
7. Berry, *Maryland's Lower Susquehanna River Valley*, 32.
8. Ibid.
9. Alsop, *Province of Maryland*, 16.
10. Weeks, *Architectural History*, 12.
11. Graves, *In the Midst*, 8.
12. Hunt, *As We Were*, 106.
13. Preston, *History of Harford County*, 52.
14. Vineyard, "Stage Waggons and Coaches."
15. Preston, *History of Harford County*, 49.
16. Vineyard, "Stage Waggons and Coaches."
17. Semmes, *Baltimore*, 30.
18. *Maryland Journal*, December 9, 1785.
19. Weeks, *Architectural History*, 14.

20. Ibid.

21. Jay, *Havre de Grace*, iv.

NINETEENTH-CENTURY LIFE IN HAVRE DE GRACE

22. Rountree, Clark and Mountford, *John Smith's Chesapeake Voyages*, 232–33.

23. Ibid., 21.

24. *Maryland Journal*, September 30, 1785.

25. Clark and Mathews, *Maryland Geological Survey*, 404.

26. Shank, "Origins," 27.

27. Weeks, *Architectural History*, 57.

28. Wilmer, *Narrative*, 6.

29. Ibid.

30. *Republican Star*, August 22, 1809.

31. *Federal Republican and Commercial Gazette*, November 6, 1810.

32. Ogden, *Rodgers Tavern*, 10.

33. Shank, "Rodgers Family," 17.

34. Hunt, *As We Were*, 53.

35. Preston, *History of Harford County*, 252.

36. MHT, HA-538.

37. Preston, *History of Harford County*, 255.

38. Ibid., 254–57.

39. Ibid.

40. Ibid.

41. William B. Stokes was the son of Robert Young Stokes, who drew the Stokes map of Havre de Grace in 1781.

42. Paullin, *Commodore John Rodgers*, 85–86.

43. MHT, HA-763.

44. Paullin, *Commodore John Rodgers*, 86.

45. Adams, *Jared Sparks*, 54–55.

46. *Federal Gazette & Baltimore Daily Advertiser*, January 3, 1798.

47. Preston, *History of Harford County*, 48.

48. Adams, *Slave Manumissions*, xi.

WHY WAR?

49. Borneman, *1812*, 19.
50. Ibid.
51. Divine, *America Past & Present*, 240.
52. *Hornet*, July 4, 1810.
53. *Niles' Weekly Register*, March 7, 1812.
54. Borneman, *1812*, 31.
55. Hunt, *As We Were*, 10–11.
56. Divine, *America Past & Present*, 243.

COMMODORE JOHN RODGERS: HOMETOWN NAVAL HERO

57. Paullin, *Commodore John Rodgers*, 19.
58. Robert Smith served as the secretary of the navy from 1801 to 1809 and was a good friend and mentor to Commodore John Rodgers.
59. Paullin, *Commodore John Rodgers*, 21.
60. Weeks, *Architectural History*, 65.
61. Paullin, *Commodore John Rodgers*, 25–26.
62. Weeks, *Architectural History*, 65.
63. Paullin, *Commodore John Rodgers*, 88.
64. Ibid., 89–90.
65. Ibid., 91.
66. Ibid., 171.
67. Ibid., 170.
68. Ibid., 172.
69. Weeks, *Architectural History*, 67.
70. Rodgers, Minerva letters, April 23, 1812.
71. Rodgers, Minerva letters, May 17, 1812.
72. Earle, *Chesapeake Bay Country*, 247.

THE BRITISH IN THE CHESAPEAKE

73. Sparks, "Conflagration," 157.
74. George, *Terror*, 29.
75. Pack, *Man Who Burned Washington*, 145–46.
76. Eshelman and Kummerow, *In Full Glory Reflected*, 29.
77. Ibid.
78. Dudley, *Naval War*, 341.
79. Ibid., 351.
80. Rodgers, Minerva letters, April 22, 1813.
81. *Niles' Weekly Register*, April 24, 1813.
82. Wilmer, *Narrative*, 10.
83. Sparks, "Conflagration," 159.
84. Ibid.
85. *Baltimore Patriot*, May 1, 1813.
86. Ibid.
87. Ibid., May 7, 1813.
88. Ibid.
89. Eshelman and Kummerow, *In Full Glory Reflected*, 30.
90. Dudley, *Naval War*, 341–42.
91. Wilmer, *Narrative*, 26.
92. Scott, *Recollections*, 99–100.
93. Mallory, *Short Stories*, 147–48.
94. Sparks, "Conflagration," 159.
95. Mallory, *Short Stories*, 149.
96. Ibid.

THE ATTACK ON HAVRE DE GRACE

97. Dudley, *Naval War*, 342.
98. Wilmer, *Narrative*, 11.
99. A fourth account of the attack was written in 1868 by Benson J. Lossing in his *Pictorial Field Book of the War of 1812*, via an interview with a Havre de Grace citizen; however, this account includes some inconsistencies.

I have decided to focus only on the details from the three first-person accounts in my retelling of the story.

100. All three of the first-person accounts of the attack on Havre de Grace refer to "the battery" singular, as does Cockburn in his letters back to Warren. Only once in Wilmer's account (page 13) does he refer to an "upper battery," giving an indication that there may have been more than one. Lossing introduces the two-battery idea, saying one battery was at Concord Point and the other "potato battery" was at mid-town. There are also some discrepancies in the various accounts on the number of guns captured by the British and their sizes. Historians have not been able to agree on whether there was one battery or two in Havre de Grace, and this issue will probably only be resolved via archaeology on the potential battery sites.

101. Mallory, *Short Stories*, 151.

102. Ibid.

103. Preston, *History of Harford County*, 243–44.

104. Latimer, *1812*, 160.

105. Eshelman and Kummerow, *In Full Glory Reflected*, 26.

106. Preston, *History of Harford County*, 243–44.

107. Scott, *Recollections*, 100–1.

108. Mallory, *Short Stories*, 151.

109. Dudley, *Naval War*, 342.

110. Wilmer, *Narrative*, 7.

111. Sparks, "Conflagration," 161.

112. Wilmer, *Narrative*, 20–21.

113. Ibid., 23–24.

114. Ibid.

115. Ibid., 15–16.

116. Ibid., 13.

117. Ibid., 17.

118. Ibid.

119. Ibid.

120. Ibid., 20.

121. Ibid., 26–27.

122. Ibid., 27.

123. Ibid., 21.

124. Ibid., 9.

125. Mallory, *Short Stories*, 152.

126. Weeks, *Architectural History*, 79.

127. Sparks, "Conflagration," 161.
128. Silver, "Lapidum," 198.
129. Ibid.
130. Dudley, *Naval War*, 343.
131. George, *Terror*, 34.
132. Dudley, *Naval War*, 343.
133. Sparks, "Conflagration," 163.

Reaction and Aftermath

134. *Baltimore Patriot*, May 4, 1813.
135. Ibid.
136. Ibid.
137. Ibid.
138. Ibid.
139. Ibid.
140. Ibid., May 5, 1813.
141. Ibid.
142. *Niles' Weekly Register*, May 8, 1813.
143. Latimer, *1812*, 160.
144. Sparks, "Conflagration," 162.
145. Wilmer, *Narrative*, 18.
146. Dudley, *Naval War*, 344.
147. Shomette, *Lost Towns*, 278.
148. Ibid., 279.
149. Ibid., 280.
150. Ibid.
151. Dudley, *Naval War*, 345.
152. Shomette, *Lost Towns*, 281.
153. George, *Terror*, 37.
154. Ibid., 53.
155. At that time, Washington was a small town and had only been the capital for fourteen years. Its moniker was "Wilderness City," and it was very sparsely populated except for the legislators. Madison and Armstrong could not believe that the city held any interest for the British, despite the fact that it was America's capital city.

The Burning of Washington

156. Eshelman and Kummerow, *In Full Glory Reflected*, 51.
157. Pack, *Man Who Burned Washington*, 13.
158. Ibid., 180.
159. Shomette, *Flotilla*, 274.
160. Eshelman and Kummerow, *In Full Glory Reflected*, 75.
161. Pack, *Man Who Burned Washington*, 14.
162. Ibid.
163. Ibid., 15.
164. Eshelman and Kummerow, *In Full Glory Reflected*, 91.
165. Pack, *Man Who Burned Washington*, 187.
166. Ibid., 16.
167. Ibid.
168. Eshelman and Kummerow, *In Full Glory Reflected*, 96.
169. Pack, *Man Who Burned Washington*, 18.
170. Standiford, *Washington Burning*, 284.
171. Ibid.
172. Ibid., 285.

The Defense of Baltimore

173. Eshelman and Kummerow, *In Full Glory Reflected*, 123.
174. Preston, *History of Harford County*, 237.
175. Lord, *Dawn's Early Light*, 235.
176. Ibid., 232.
177. Eshelman and Kummerow, *In Full Glory Reflected*, 128.
178. George, "Harford County," 40.
179. Ibid., 44.
180. Ibid.
181. Lord, *Dawn's Early Light*, 252.
182. George, "Harford County," 46.
183. Weeks, *Architectural History*, 69.
184. Eshelman and Kummerow, *In Full Glory Reflected*, 130.
185. Ibid., 146.

186. Key, *Defense of Fort McHenry*.
187. George, "Harford County," 60.
188. Ibid.

REBUILDING HAVRE DE GRACE

189. Mallory, *Short Stories*, 154.
190. Preston, *History of Harford County*, 260.
191. Ibid.
192. MHT, HA-798.
193. Ibid., HA-788.
194. Ibid., HA-544.
195. Ibid., HA-796.
196. Ibid., HA-537.
197. The Havre de Grace Visitor's Center offers a self-guided walking tour of the historic homes in town. Visitors can pick up "The Lafayette Trail" brochure at the Visitor's Center (711 Pennington Avenue) and visit most of these historic homes on foot.
198. MHT, HA-790.
199. Ibid.
200. Ibid., HA-809.
201. Ibid., HA-111.
202. Ibid., HA-835, HA-832, HA-830.
203. Weeks, *Architectural History*, 367.
204. Wright, *Our Harford Heritage*, 317.
205. Ibid.
206. Weeks, *Architectural History*, 70.
207. Ibid.
208. George, *Terror*, 34.
209. MHT, CE-112A.
210. Weeks, *Architectural History*, 81. Bloomsbury no longer stands. It was located on the land where today's Havre de Grace Activity Center in located on Lewis Lane.
211. Shomette, *Lost Towns*, 258.
212. Ibid.
213. Wright, *Our Harford Heritage*, 121.
214. Ibid., 124.

215. Jay, *Havre de Grace*, 99.
216. MHT, HA-548.
217. Ibid., HA-546 and HA-1122.
218. Wright, *Our Harford Heritage*, 145.
219. Ibid., 314.
220. MHT, HA-1099.
221. Ibid., HA-543.
222. Ibid., HA-542.
223. Ibid., HA-815.
224. Ibid., HA-1107.
225. Ibid., HA-549.

BIBLIOGRAPHY

Adams, Carolyn Greenfield. *Hunter Sutherland's Slave Manumissions and Sales in Harford County, Maryland 1775–1865.* Bowie, MD: Heritage Books Inc., 1999.

Adams, Herbert B. *The Life and Writings of Jared Sparks: Comprising Selections from His Journals and Correspondence.* Boston: Houghton, Mifflin and Company, 1893.

Alsop, George. *Character of the Province of Maryland. 1638.* Accessed at mith.umd.edu/eada/html/display.php?docs=alsop_character.xml&action=show, June 28, 2012.

Baltimore Metropolitan Council. *Transportation System Development in the Baltimore Region and Maryland. (2005).* Accessed at www.baltometro.org/reports/TransSysDevelopment.pdf, August 6, 2012.

Baltimore Patriot. April 29, 1813. Accessed via America's Historical Newspapers, May 15, 2012.

———. May 1, 1813. Accessed via America's Historical Newspapers, May 15, 2012.

———. May 4, 1813. Accessed via America's Historical Newspapers, December 1, 2011.

———. May 5, 1813. Accessed via America's Historical Newspapers, February 17, 2012.

———. May 6, 1813. Accessed via America's Historical Newspapers, December 1, 2011.

———. May 7, 1813. Accessed via America's Historical Newspapers, April 16, 2012.

———. "Testimony of Publick Respect." January 16, 1813. Accessed via America's Historical Newspapers, May 15, 2012.

Bartgis, Matthias E. *Journal of Captain Matthias E. Bartgis, 16th Regiment, September 1814*. N.p.: Maryland Historical Society MS, 1913.

Berry, David A. *Maryland's Lower Susquehanna River Valley: Where the River Meets the Bay*. Charleston, SC: The History Press, 2009.

Borneman, Walter R. *1812: The War That Forged a Nation*. New York: HarperCollins, 2004.

Boston Daily Advertiser. May 10, 1813. Accessed via America's Historical Newspapers, December 1, 2011.

Brugger, Robert J. *Maryland: A Middle Temperament 1634–1980*. Baltimore, MD: Johns Hopkins University Press, 1988.

Carter, Edward C., II, ed. *The Papers of Benjamin Henry Latrobe. Volume 3 1799–1820: From Philadelphia to New Orleans*. New Haven, CT: Yale University Press, 1980.

Clark, William Bullock, and Edward Bennett Mathews. *Maryland Geological Survey Report*. Vol. 2. 1898. Accessed at books.google.com/books?id=_8dL AAAAMAAJ&pg=PA497&lpg=PA497&dq=haudecoeur+map+havre+d e+grace&source=bl&ots=NEIg0O_gWW&sig=U68EoSuFLeQ2d7Poeo_ XCOmpgoI&hl=en&sa=X&ei=VHQlUPbLBvKz0QGI1oGoDA&ved= 0CEAQ6AEwAA#v=onepage&q=haudecoeur%20map%20havre%20 de%20grace&f=false, August 10, 2012.

Commercial Advertiser. May 5, 1813. Accessed via America's Historical Newspapers, February 17, 2012.

Divine, Robert A., et al. *America Past & Present Volume 1: To 1877.* New York: Pearson Education, Inc., 2007.

Dudley, William S., ed. *The Naval War of 1812: A Documentary History.* Washington, D.C.: Naval Historical Center, 1992.

Earle, Swepson. *The Chesapeake Bay Country.* New York: Weathervane Books, 1923.

Eshelman, Ralph E. *A Travel Guide to the War of 1812 in the Chesapeake.* Baltimore, MD: Johns Hopkins University Press, 2011.

Eshelman, Ralph, and Burt Kummerow. *In Full Glory Reflected: Discovering the War of 1812 in the Chesapeake.* Marceline, MO: Walsworth Publishing Company, 2012.

Federal Gazette & Baltimore Daily Advertiser. January 3, 1798. Accessed via America's Historical Newspapers, February 17, 2012.

————. "Mill Seats." October 29, 1801. Accessed via America's Historical Newspapers, December 1, 2011.

————. "20 Dollars Reward." January 3, 1798. Accessed via America's Historical Newspapers, December 1, 2011.

Federal Republican. "A Farm for Sale." February 18, 1812. Baltimore, MD. Accessed via America's Historical Newspapers, May 15, 2012.

————. "Public Sale." March 19, 1812. Baltimore, MD. Accessed via America's Historical Newspapers, May 15, 2012.

Federal Republican & Commercial Gazette. November 6, 1810. Baltimore, MD. Accessed via America's Historical Newspapers, February 17, 2012.

————. "To the Public." November 6, 1810. Baltimore, MD. Accessed via America's Historical Newspapers, December 1, 2011.

George, Christopher T. "Harford County in the War of 1812." *Harford Historical Bulletin* 76 (Spring 1998).

————. *Terror on the Chesapeake: The War of 1812 on the Bay*. Shippensburg, PA: White Mane Books, 2000.

Graves, Dianne. *In the Midst of Alarms: The Untold Story of Women and the War of 1812*. Cap-Saint-Ignace, Quebec: Robin Brass Studio, 2007.

Graves, Donald E. *Sir William Congreve and the Rocket's Red Glare*. Ontario: Museum Restoration Service, 1989.

Hagers-town Gazette. April 27, 1813. Accessed via America's Historical Newspapers, May 15, 2012.

Hickey, Donald R. In *In Full Glory Reflected: Discovering the War of 1812 in the Chesapeake*, Ralph Eshelman and Burt Kummerow. Marceline, MO: Walsworth Publishing Company, 2012.

The Hornet. July 4, 1810. Fredericktown, MD. Accessed via America's Historical Newspapers, December 1, 2011.

Hunt, Gaillard. *As We Were: Life in America 1814*. Stockbridge, MA: Berkshire House Publishing, 1993.

Jay, Peter A. *Havre de Grace: An Informal History*. Havre de Grace, MD: Sparrowhawk Press, 1994.

Key, Francis Scott. *The Defense of Fort McHenry*. N.p., 1814.

Latimer, Jon. *1812: War with America*. Cambridge, MA: Belknap Press of Harvard University Press, 2007.

Lord, Walter. *The Dawn's Early Light*. Baltimore, MD: Johns Hopkins University Press, 1972.

Lossing, Benson J. *Pictorial Field Book of the War of 1812*. New York: Harper & Brothers, 1869.

Mallory, Daniel. *Short Stories and Reminiscences of the Last Fifty Years. By an Old Traveler*. 1842. Accessed on Library of Congress website, December 22, 2011.

Maryland Gazette. September 16, 1790. Annapolis, MD. Accessed via America's Historical Newspapers, December 1, 2011.

Maryland Historical Trust/District Maryland Historical Trust Internal NR-Eligibility Review Form. HA-526 Mount Felix, 1991.

Maryland Historical Trust Survey. No. CE-112A Principio Iron Works Company Office, 1970.

————. No. CE-129 Rodgers Tavern, 1970.

————. No. HA-9 Oakington, 1969.

————. No. HA-111 Motz House, 1977.

————. No. HA-242 Belle Vue Farm, 1977.

————. No. HA-526 Mount Felix, 1976.

————. No. HA-537 Old Ordinary, 1977.

————. No. HA-538 Market Place, 1970.

————. No. HA-542 Silverstein House, 1976.

————. No. HA-543 Carver-Coburn House, 1976.

————. No. HA-544 St. John's Episcopal Church, 1976.

————. No. HA-546 Hall House (Mathias-Courtney House), 1977.

————. No. HA-547 Thomas Hopkins House, 1976.

————. No. HA-548 Sappington House, 1976.

———. No. HA-549 Spencer-Silver Mansion, 1977.

———. No. HA-763–764 Mount Pleasant, 1991.

———. No. HA-788 Aveilhe-Goldborough House, 1977.

———. No. HA-790 Abraham Jarrett Thomas House (Lafayette Hotel), 1977.

———. No. HA-793 Poplar House, 1977.

———. No. HA-795 Barnes-Boyd House, 1977.

———. No. HA-796 Joshua Green House, 1977.

———. No. HA-798 Elizabeth Rodgers House, 1977.

———. No. HA-807 Joseph Carver House, 1977.

———. No. HA-808 Nicolas and Gabriel Sutor House, 1977.

———. No. HA-809 John O'Neill House, 1977.

———. No. HA-815 Seneca Mansion, 1977.

———. No. HA-822 Lauretta Harris House, 1976.

———. No. HA-826 Riffle House, 1976.

———. No. HA-830 McCabe House, 1976.

———. No. HA-832 Barnes-Hopper House, 1976.

———. No. HA-835 Wollen Double House, 1976.

———. No. HA-1095 Lawder-Willis House, 1976.

———. No. HA-1099 James Hopper House, 1976.

———. No. HA-1107 Vandiver Mansion, 1986.

———. No. HA-1116 Putland House, 1977.

———. No. HA-1122 Hoke House, 1976.

———. No. HA-1131 Foard Double House, 1977.

———. No. HA-1163 Beachley House, 1977.

Maryland Journal. December 9, 1785. Baltimore, MD. Accessed via America's Historical Newspapers, December 1, 2011.

———. February 28, 1786. Baltimore, MD. Accessed via America's Historical Newspapers, January 14, 2011.

———. January 13, 1786. Baltimore, MD. Accessed via America's Historical Newspapers, January 14, 2011.

———. September 30, 1785. Baltimore, MD. Accessed via America's Historical Newspapers, December 1, 2011.

———. "Thoughts of the Subject of State Roads." December 9, 1785. Accessed via America's Historical Newspapers, January 14, 2011.

Montgomery, Dennis. "Captain John Smith." *Colonial Williamsburg Journal* (Spring 1994). Accessed www.history.org/foundation/journal/smith.cfm, August 6, 2012.

National Advocate. May 10, 1813. Accessed via America's Historical Newspapers, December 1, 2011.

National Register of Historic Places Inventory: Nomination Form. HA-251 Havre de Grace Lighthouse, 1975.

———. HA-538 Site of Market House, n.d.

———. HA-812 Harford Memorial (Hospital) School of Practical Membership (the old E.C. Wells House), n.d.

New York Gazette and General Advertiser. May 7, 1813. Accessed via America's

Historical Newspapers, December 1, 2011.

———. May 8, 1813. Accessed via America's Historical Newspapers, December 1, 2011.

Niles' Weekly Register 2, no. 1 (March 7, 1812), 5.

——— 4 (April 24, 1813), 134, 164.

Ogden, Ashley G. *The Rodgers Tavern Story*. Cecil County, MD: Society for the Preservation of Maryland Antiquities, 1968. In the files of the Maryland Historical Society.

Pack, James. *The Man Who Burned Washington: Admiral Sir George Cockburn 1772–1853*. London: Redwood Burn Limited, 1987.

Paullin, Charles Oscar. *Commodore John Rodgers, Captain, Commodore and Senior Officer of the American Navy 1773–1838*. Annapolis, MD: United States Naval Institute, 1967.

Preston, Walter W.A.M. *History of Harford County, Maryland from 1608 (The Year of Smith's Exploration) to the Close of the War of 1812*. Baltimore, MD: Regional Publishing Company, 1901.

Principio to Sparrows Point: A Brief History of Maryland's Iron Industry Part 1 and Part 2. Maryland Historical Society MTN 703.B56.

Quesenbery, Erika L. *History of Port Deposit*. www.portdeposit.org/?a=history_ detail, August 6, 2012.

Republican Star. August 22, 1809. Easton, MD. Accessed via American Historical Newspapers, February 17, 2011.

———. May 11, 1813. Easton, MD. Accessed via American Historical Newspapers, February 17, 2011.

———. "To Be Rented." August 22, 1809. Easton, MD. Accessed via America's Historical Newspapers, December 1, 2011.

Rodgers, John. "John Rodgers, a Biographical Sketch." Manuscript,

Maryland Historical Society, 1846.

Rodgers, Minerva. *Rodgers Family Papers*. Library of Congress.

Rountree, Helen C., Wayne E. Clark and Kevin Mountford. *John Smith's Chesapeake Voyages 1607–1609*. Charlottesville: University of Virginia Press, 2007.

Scott, James. *Recollections of a Naval Life*. 3 vols. London: Richard Bentley, 1834.

Semmes, Raphael. *Baltimore as Seen by Visitors 1783–1860*. Baltimore: Maryland Historical Society, 1953.

Shank, Ellsworth. "Origins of the Street Names of Havre de Grace." *Harford Historical Bulletin* 24 (Spring 1985): 27–32.

————. "The Rodgers Family and Havre de Grace." *Harford Historical Bulletin* 24 (Spring 1985): 17–21.

Shomette, Donald G. *Flotilla: The Patuxent Naval Campaign in the War of 1812*. Baltimore, MD: Johns Hopkins University Press, 2009.

————. *Lost Towns of Tidewater Maryland*. Centreville, MD: Tidewater Publishers, 2000.

Silver, Albert Peter. "Lapidum: A Chapter of Harford County History." *Bel Air Times*, Bel Air, MD, 1932.

Smith, John. In *Captain John Smith: A Select Edition of His Writings*, edited by Karen Ordahl Kupperman. Chapel Hill: University of North Carolina Press, 1988. Accessed via explorepahistory.com/odocument. php?docId=1-4-F0, August 14, 2012.

Sparks, Jared. "Conflagration of Havre de Grace." *North American Review and Miscellaneous Journal* 14, no. 5 (July 1817).

Standiford, Les. *Washington Burning*. New York: Random House, 2008.

Thomas A. Hays Papers, War of 1812—Militia, Archives of the Historical Society of Harford County.

Tilp, Frederick. *The Chesapeake Bay of Yore: Mainly about the Rowing and Sailing Craft.* Annapolis, MD: Chesapeake Bay Foundation, 1982.

U.S. Department of Transportation, Federal Highway Administration. "Highway History." Accessed via www.fhwa.dot.gov/highwayhistory/us1pr.cfm, September 1, 2012.

Vineyard, Ron. "Stage Waggons and Coaches." Colonial Williamsburg Foundation Library Research Report Series. Williamsburg, VA, 2000. Accessed via research.history.org/DigitalLibrary/View/index.cfm?doc=ResearchReports\RR0380.xml, July 8, 2012.

Weeks, Christopher. *An Architectural History of Harford County, Maryland.* Baltimore, MD: Johns Hopkins University Press, 1996.

Wilmer, James Jones. *Narrative Respecting the Conduct of the British from Their First Landing on Specutia Island Till Their Progress to Havre de Grace…By a Citizen of Havre de Grace.* Baltimore, MD: P. Mauro, 1813.

Wright, C. Milton. *Our Harford Heritage: A History of Harford County, Maryland.* Glen Burnie, MD: French-Bay Printing Company, 1967.

INDEX

ABOUT THE AUTHOR

Heidi L. Glatfelter is the founder and president of Market Early America, a consulting business where she helps history museums with marketing, communications, technology, exhibits, research and interpretation. She also runs the website History Site Locator (www.historysitelocator.com), which is a searchable database of history museums across the country. She has been working since November 2010 with the Heritage Museums of Havre de Grace on a multi-site exhibit that tells the story of the British attack on the town, and this book grew out of that project. In her spare time, she enjoys spoiling her dog, reading, sewing and, of course, history. You can learn more about Heidi's professional pursuits at www.marketearlyamerica.com.

Photo by Phil Romans.

Visit us at
www.historypress.net